ENJOY!

CHEF
DEZ

*Chef*
*Dez*
*on Cooking*

*Volume 2*

Order this book online at www.trafford.com
or email orders@trafford.com

Most Trafford titles are also available at major online book retailers.

Note for Librarians: A cataloguing record for this book is available from Library
and Archives Canada at www.collectionscanada.ca/amicus/index-e.html

Printed in Victoria, BC, Canada.

ISBN: 978-1-4269-1864-3

*Our mission is to efficiently provide the world's finest, most comprehensive book publishing
service, enabling every author to experience success. To find out how to publish your book, your
way, and have it available worldwide, visit us online at www.trafford.com*

*Trafford rev. 10/22/2009*

**Trafford** PUBLISHING® www.trafford.com

**North America & international**
toll-free: 1 888 232 4444 (USA & Canada)
phone: 250 383 6864 ♦ fax: 812 355 4082

For my Mom, Angie...

the spark that started this flame

*T*

To reduce the cost of this book to you, the consumer, colour photos for the following recipes available for viewing/printing on my website at:

*www.chefdez.com*

Apple & Cinnamon Topped Pancakes
Basil Ricotta Pasta Filling
BC Birthday Cobb Salad
Big Pockets for My Sole
Black Forest Tiramisu
Blueberry Bran Muffins
Blueberry Salsa
Cajun Flank Steak with Grits
Cajun Pork Tenderloin
Corn, Date & Goat Cheese Salad
Drunken Pig
Dublin Coddle
Easiest Mussels Recipe Ever
Fiery Asian Grilled Pork Chops
Fresh Pasta From Scratch
Garlic Gewurztraminer Fudge
Grilled Blueberry Brie Chicken Sandwich

Hold My Chipotle Beer Pasta
Homemade Muesli
Hop 'n Shrimp Gumbo
Irish Soda Bread
Kristal's Sweet Chili Lime Seafood Medley
Louisiana Red Beans & Rice
Merlot Sauced Steak Sandwiches
Minestrone
My Dad's Famous Chipotle Spaghetti Sauce
Nothin But Love Indian Caesar Appy
Oatmeal Breakfast Bars
Pan Seared Scallops in Sage Brown Butter
Pastry Wrapped Herbes de Provence Camembert
Patricia's Mediterranean Chicken
Peach & Thyme Pork Chops
Peppered Cheese Bread
Peppersteak Madagascar
Pineapple Salsa
Pralines with Sweet Biscuits & Rum Flambéed Bananas
Prawn & Veggie Kabobs
Roasted Pepper Eggs Benedict
Rumbledethumps
Saucy Little Meat Loaves
Scotch Eggs
Scottish Dundee Cake with Scotch Infused Whip Cream
Spiced Apple Loaf
Spicy Fennel Nuts
The World's Best Cornbread
Tomato & Sausage Clams
Tomato Basil Pasta Sauce
Whole Wheat Graham Crackers

# *Acknowledgments*

With just over two years since the release of my first book *Chef Dez on Cooking Volume One* I am very pleased to bring you this second volume. My original goal was not to have *Chef Dez on Cooking Volume Two* published so soon, but we have received so many compliments on the first volume that the demand for this second book made it an obvious choice. What you are holding in your hands is a labour of love from me and my wife Katherine. Bringing a cookbook together is not an easy task, but our shared passion for food and cooking with each other has made the journey very enjoyable.

This being said, she is the first person I need to thank. The progress of this book has seen the birth of our daughter Gianna, busy times raising a family, and the constant pursuit of our careers, but yet she has never let me down. The support and dedication she has given me during this project has never waned, and I am so grateful. She again has a chapter dedicated to her talent in baking - you will find that *"Chapter 10 – Quick Breads are Named for their Convenience"* includes only recipes of hers. Katherine, you are the most amazing woman and best friend. Thank you so much for everything you are and everything you do.

My four incredible children, Corey, Krista, Noah, and Gianna, are also loves of my life, and the pride that I have for you as a Father makes everything I do so worthwhile. It is always challenging to keep a balanced life and my goal, even in my busiest times, is to be the best dad that I can be to you. Thank you for your understanding and patience during the making of this book.

To whom this book is dedicated to, I cannot forget to mention my Mom. The passion that I have for food, that enlightens every part of my life today, was ignited by her since I was a young boy. We have been through a lot together and I can always count on her for encouragement in any venture I am pursuing. Mom, you are an incredible person and an amazing Grammy to your Grandchildren. I honestly believe that because of your overflowing unbiased kindness, you touch the souls of everyone you meet. I look forward to many more years together.

*Limbert Mountain Farm* in Agassiz, BC is not just another venue that I teach at. Claude and Trudie have become good friends who I always look forward to seeing and spending evenings with, eating good food, drinking wine, and sharing great stories with each other. Thank you for being such a huge supporter of me and for writing the foreword of this book.

Angie at Well Seasoned Gourmet Food Store in Langley, BC has also gone above and beyond in supporting everything I do. From not only booking me numerous times teaching in her incredible store, but also hosting my book launches, and including me in so many ventures – like being the MC at the annual BBQ on the By-Pass, for example. Thank you Angie.

Other venues that I teach at deserve recognition as well, such as Dan & Darlene at Once Upon a Vine, Remco at Neat Freakz, and Mission Parks & Recreation.

Gratitude to all of the venues I have performed shows at over the past two years: West Coast Women's Show, Ridge Meadows Home Show, Chilliwack Exhibition, The Town of Kapuskasing, Kapestro's Restaurant, and especially the Abbotsford Agrifair where I perform 16 shows every year during the August long weekend.

A great appreciation also to the following: Trafford Publishing, Wendy Gilmour of Gilmour Promotions, my Dad (Dez Senior) for his famous Chipotle Spaghetti recipe, Bill Androsiuk, Anna Cavaliere, CanWest Broadcasting, Weber Shandwick, all of my family & friends, Katherine's family, and all of the Editors and Publishers of *Chef Dez on Cooking* for the ongoing support they have given me.

Lastly, I want to thank my regular clients and everyone who has attended my classes, welcomed me into their homes, attended my cooking shows, bought my first book, and has been a dedicated reader of my columns. Without you… none of this would be a reality. Thank you so very much.

# Table of Contents

*A*lthough we have been growers of organic produce for over 30 years, it was only a few years ago that we decided to enlarge our farm and open it to the public. We built a commercial kitchen in our barn, and decided to make it large enough to seat 20 people so we could not only process food products, but also use it as a teaching kitchen.

The problem was that we didn't have a qualified 'teacher.' We contacted Dez, and began a 3-year relationship that has grown into a friendship. We have shared many afternoons and evenings assisting him as he shares his passion for food, family, and fun with hundreds of food lovers.

As growers of over 60 varieties of culinary herbs, we have watched Dez adapt from 'store bought' to 'fresh grown,' much to the delight of those tasting his meals. Perhaps the best class was 'Surprise the Chef' night. We supplied only fresh local ingredients, and Dez had only 2 hours before the class started to create a menu. The results were fantastic and greatly appreciated by all.

What we admire most about Dez is that he sees cooking as a journey, to be explored and enjoyed, not a chore. He continually broadens his range of gastronomical experience, which he shares with us through his food columns, cooking shows and classes. For our classes he has prepared many of the recipes in his first book, *Chef Dez on Cooking Volume One,* and we have found them to be simple to follow, and the results are always delicious. We are really looking forward to *Volume Two.*

Congratulations on your new book Dez, We are privileged and honored to be able to introduce it to all those fortunate enough to be reading this.

*Trudie and Claude Bouchard*

*Simply Fine Foods at Limbert Mountain Farm*

*www.limbertmountainfarm.com*

# 1

## Black Beer for St. Patrick's Day

My annual salute to the Irish always includes a pint of Guinness Beer, a delicious black stout from Dublin, Ireland. This full-bodied beer has a considerably smooth finish despite its bold characteristics, and is delightful to drink anytime of the year. Although there are many fans of this traditional ale, there are just as many cynics due to its dominant taste. I have determined however that even people, who don't drink beer or alcohol, can appreciate the unique taste of Guinness when used in cooking.

I always question a recipe when it calls for water to be added. Why not add wine, broth, juice, or even beer? How much flavour does water have? Zero. If you want a dish to taste wonderful, and full of flavour, could you not add something that has more distinction than water? I always address this topic to my culinary students and preach creativity and improvisation when it comes to preparing a meal. Guinness beer is a very clever way to add flavour intricacy to a dish, especially when the recipe involves red meat. The hearty flavour of red meat holds up nicely when married with the boldness of Guinness, whereas the taste of fish would most likely be lost.

A beef stew, for example, made with a combination of beef broth and Guinness beer is incredible. The full-flavoured dark, almost black, broth will not only have them guessing, but it will also have them requesting a second helping! With this knowledge in hand, think of the endless possibilities of recipe modifications you can now carry out. Try Guinness in beef gravy, Sheppard's pie, casseroles, soups, stroganoff, or even your next beef and tomato spaghetti sauce, to name a few. You can even try marinating an inexpensive, tough cut of beef in Guinness. You will be amazed at the results.

The flavour and darkness of this beer comes from the selected hops and roasting of malt barley, similar to the way coffee beans are roasted. Although Guinness representatives claim that the colour of their beer is actually a deep ruby red, black is popularly used to describe the obscurity of this beer here in Canada. The smoothness is supposedly from the pure water obtained from natural springs fed by the St. James well.

In modern day Ireland, St. Patrick's Day has traditionally been celebrated as a religious holiday. It was up until the 1970's that Irish law banned the opening of pubs on the 17th of March. So this St. Patrick's Day, one may find it more fitting to raise your fork or spoon (instead of a glass) in a toast to St. Patrick, the Patron Saint of Ireland. However, let's also make a point of remembering Arthur Guinness, who set up his brewery in Dublin, Ireland in 1759, by signing a nine thousand year lease. Thank you Arthur!

*Dear Chef Dez:*

*Where does the alcohol go when you reduce wine (beer) during the cooking process? I assume it's still in the pan, but not in sufficient quantities to worry about. Is this correct?*

*Larry P.*
*Ladner, BC*

*Dear Larry:*

*Yes, a minimal amount of alcohol is left in the pan but not enough to be concerned about, as long as it boils for a period of time. Alcohol is lighter than water and evaporates out of the pan. This will always happen when you are "reducing" to increase flavour - if water is evaporating, you can be certain that the alcohol is as well.*

# Colcannon

*"A classic Irish side dish made with basic staple ingredients. Best served with Guinness Cream Sauce."*

4 extra-large russet potatoes, peeled and diced one-half inch
5 cups shredded (or thinly sliced) green cabbage
1 small onion, diced small
6 large cloves of garlic, minced
¾ (three quarters) cup butter
4 tsp salt
1 tsp pepper
¾ (three quarters) cup whipping cream
Fresh chopped parsley, for garnish

1. Steam the diced potatoes over boiling water until tender, approximately 20 minutes.
2. While the potatoes are steaming, melt ¼ (one quarter) cup of the butter in a large pan over medium heat until it just starts foaming. Add the cabbage, onion, garlic and 1 tsp of the salt to the pan and cook until mostly soft, while stirring occasionally. Approximately 15 minutes.
3. Cube the remaining ½ (one half) cup butter and add it to the steamed potatoes along with the other 3 tsp salt and the 1 tsp pepper. Mash until thoroughly combined.
4. Stir the cabbage mixture and cream into the potatoes until thoroughly combined. Taste and re-season if necessary.
5. Serve immediately with Guinness Cream Sauce.

*Make approximately 6 to 10 side portions*

# Dublin Coddle

Full colour photo available at www.chefdez.com

*"Rustic Irish cooking at its best! This classic casserole is made up of potatoes and sausages and baked to perfection with a combination of chicken broth, cream and Guinness beer."*

12 large pork, beef or Italian sausages
4 extra-large russet potatoes, peeled and sliced very thin
8 bacon strips, sliced into ¼ (one quarter) inch pieces
4 medium onions, chopped
6 cloves of garlic, finely chopped
1 tbsp salt
1 tsp sugar
1 tsp dried sage
Pepper
½ (one half) cup chicken broth
½ (one half) cup whipping cream
½ (one half) cup Guinness beer
Finely chopped parsley, for garnish

1. Heat large non-stick pan over medium heat. Add the sausages and cook until browned on all sides, approximately 8 to 12 minutes. Set sausages aside and discard the fat from the pan.
2. While the sausages are cooking, preheat oven to 350 degrees, and arrange potato slices into a large casserole dish, or preferably a large ceramic coated cast iron pot.
3. Return the pan to the stove and increase the heat to medium-high. Add the bacon, onions, garlic, salt, sugar, sage and season with pepper. Cook until the onions are soft and slightly browned, approximately 5 to 10 minutes.
4. Spread this onion/bacon mixture evenly over the potato slices.
5. Pour the broth, cream and beer over the entire dish.
6. Place the sausages on top. Cover and cook for 1 hour in the preheated oven.
7. Sprinkle with the chopped parsley and serve "family style", by dishing it out at the table.

*Serves 6 to 8 people.*

# Guinness Beef Stew

*"A combination of Guinness, red wine and beef broth makes a deliciously complex broth for the hearty stew. Thickening the stew is optional."*

4 tbsp canola oil
1 kg cubed beef chuck stewing meat
Salt & pepper
4 medium carrots, ½ to ¾ inch coins
2 celery stalks, sliced
1 medium onion, diced small
6 garlic cloves, chopped small
2 stalks fresh rosemary, chopped
3 bay leaves
1 – 440ml can of Guinness beer
1 cup full bodied red wine
1 cup beef broth
2 tbsp dark brown sugar
2 large red-skinned potatoes, diced ½ to ¾ inch
2 tbsp cornstarch with a few tbsp red wine, optional

1.  Heat a heavy bottomed large pot over medium high heat.
2.  Toss the stew meat with 1 tablespoon of the oil and salt & pepper.
3.  Add the other 3 tablespoons of oil to the heated pot. Brown the stew pieces in the hot oil – making sure not to overcrowd the pot. As the pieces are browned, remove and set aside.
4.  Lower the heat to medium and add the carrot, celery, onion, garlic, rosemary and more salt & pepper. Cook for approximately 2 minutes until the vegetables have softened a bit.
5.  Add the bay leaves, Guinness, wine, broth, brown sugar, potatoes, and the reserved browned stew meat. Bring to a boil and then cover, reduce the heat to low and simmer for 1.5 to 2 hours until the meat is tender. Season to taste with salt & pepper and serve.
6.  **Optional – if you want a thicker broth – mix the cornstarch with the few tablespoons of wine and stir it into the finished stew. Bring to a boil to thicken and then serve.

*Makes 6 to 8 portions*

# Guinness Cream Sauce

*"Fantastic on classic Irish Colcannon. Rich, flavourful and leave a finishing taste of Guinness on the palate."*

1 ¾ (one and three quarters) cups beef broth
3 tbsp cornstarch
¾ (three quarters) cup Guinness beer
¼ (one quarter) cup dark brown sugar
1 tsp salt
½ (one half) tsp pepper
2 garlic cloves, crushed
¾ (three quarters) cup whipping cream

1.  In a small bowl, mix ¼ (one quarter) cup of the beef broth with the cornstarch. Set aside.
2.  In a medium heavy-bottomed pot, combine the rest of the beef broth with the beer, sugar, salt, pepper, and garlic. Heat to boiling over medium-high heat. Once boiling, reduce the heat down to medium-low and simmer for 10 minutes.
3.  Add the cream and cornstarch mixture and whisk to combine. Increase the heat to medium-high and continue whisking constantly until it comes to a full boil and thickens. Remove from heat and serve.

*Makes approximately 3 cups*

# Guinness Shepherd's Pie

*"A classic Irish pub favourite! Shepherd's Pie made with ground beef instead of the traditional ground lamb is actually called a Cottage Pie, but I kept the name Shepherd's Pie because it is more recognizable."*

4 large russet potatoes, peeled and diced ½ inch
2 pounds (908g) lean ground beef
1 cup small diced onion

1 cup small diced carrot

1 cup small diced celery

6 garlic cloves, minced

¼ (one quarter) cup flour

1 tbsp dried oregano

1 tbsp dried thyme

2 tsp salt

1 tsp pepper

1.5 tsp beef stock paste

1 – 156ml can tomato paste

1 – 440ml can Guinness beer

2 tbsp sugar

1 tbsp Worcestershire sauce

1 cup frozen peas

½ (one half) cup butter, cubed

2 tsp salt

½ (one half) tsp pepper

1 egg

¼ (one quarter) cup whipping cream

1.  Preheat the oven to 400 degrees.
2.  Steam the potatoes for 20 minutes or until tender, set aside but keep warm over the water.
3.  While the potatoes are steaming, brown the beef in a large pan over medium heat until all the liquid from the beef has evaporated, approximately 15 to 20 minutes.
4.  To the beef, add the onion, carrot, celery, garlic, flour, oregano, thyme, 2 tsp salt, and 1 tsp pepper. Cook until softened a bit, approximately 5 to 7 minutes.
5.  Stir in the beef stock paste and tomato paste until evenly distributed.
6.  Stir in the Guinness, sugar, Worcestershire, and peas. Taste and re-season with salt and pepper if necessary. Remove from heat and let stand while mashing the potatoes.
7.  Add the butter, 2 tsp salt, and ½ tsp pepper to the steamed potatoes and mash together until smooth.
8.  In a small bowl thoroughly beat the egg and whipping cream together. Slowly add this to the mashed potatoes while incorporating to ensure

that the egg doesn't become scrambled. Taste and re-season with salt and pepper if necessary.

9.  Put the beef mixture into a 9 x 13 inch cake pan or casserole dish. Top evenly with the mashed potatoes and run a fork over the potatoes to make a design.

10.  Bake for 30 minutes until the potato starts to brown. Rest 10-20 minutes before serving.

*Makes approximately 8 to 12 portions*

# Hold My Chipotle Beer Pasta

**Full colour photo available at www.chefdez.com**

*"I wrote this recipe for country Artist Aaron Pritchett. Canned chipotle peppers are usually found in the Mexican section of any major grocery store – and contain at least 4 to 6 peppers per can"*

3 tbsp canola oil
680g (1.5 pounds) chicken breast filets, cut into bite-sized pieces
Salt & pepper
1 medium onion, finely diced
6 to 8 garlic cloves, minced
2 ½ (two and one half) tsp salt
½ (one half) tsp pepper
2 – 796ml (28 fl oz.) cans diced tomatoes, drained
156ml (5.5 fl oz.) can tomato paste
2 tbsp white sugar
1 tbsp dried oregano leaves
1 tbsp dried thyme leaves
2 chipotle peppers (canned), minced
440ml can Guinness beer, or other dark stout
375g-package whole-wheat linguine pasta
Fresh parsley, chopped fine, for garnish

1.  Heat a heavy-bottomed pan over medium-high heat.

2. Add the canola oil and the chicken pieces and season lightly with salt & pepper. Stir occasionally until browned and cooked through.

3. Remove chicken with a slotted spoon.

4. Reduce the heat to medium – add the onions, then the garlic and the salt & pepper. Cook 2 to 3 minutes until soft, stirring occasionally.

5. Add the drained tomatoes, tomato paste, sugar, oregano, thyme, and chipotle peppers. Stir to combine.

6. Add the beer. Increase the heat to medium-high and bring to a boil.

7. Reduce the heat and simmer uncovered until the sauce reaches desired consistency, approximately 5 minutes.

8. While sauce is reducing, cook pasta according to package instructions.

9. Stir chicken pieces into the sauce. Toss in the cooked pasta and serve immediately, garnished with chopped parsley.

*Makes 4 to 6 portions*

# Irish Soda Bread

**Full colour photo available at www.chefdez.com**

*"Not made with Guinness, but this bread compliments any Irish meal"*

2 ¾ (two and three quarters) cups all-purpose flour
¼ (one quarter) cup wheat germ
3 tablespoons white sugar
1 tsp baking soda
1 tsp baking powder
½ (one half) tsp salt
¼ (one quarter) cup butter, in small cubes
1 ½ (one and one half) cups buttermilk

1. Preheat the oven to 375 degrees. Prepare a baking sheet with baking spray or parchment paper.

2. In a large bowl, combine the flour, wheat germ, sugar, baking soda, baking powder and salt.

3. Cut in the butter into this mixture until the butter pieces are approximately pea sized.

4. Add the buttermilk and stir until it just starts to come together.

5. Empty contents onto a lightly floured surface and gently press the dough together until it starts to become smooth and resembles a flattened ball approximately 1 ½ (one and one half) inches thick. Do not over work the dough or it will become tough.

6. Gently transfer the dough round onto the prepared baking sheet. With a floured knife, cut an "x" across the top of the dough.

7. Bake for approximately 40 to 45 minutes until golden, and a toothpick inserted into the center of the loaf comes out dry.

8. Cool on a wire rack. Cut into wedges just prior to serving.

*Makes 1 eight-inch round loaf*

# 2

## Gourmet Picnic Ideas

How many people are tired of the same old picnics items? Do memories of bland potato salads and boring sandwiches persuade you to buy fast food or, worse yet, keep you locked indoors? Whether it's a romantic picnic for two, or a family outing, easy to prepare gourmet ideas will liven-up your picnic basket.

One of the simplest things to pack for a romantic picnic for two is a fruit and cheese assortment, as there is virtually no preparation required. A grocery store with a delicatessen counter will be able to provide you with a number of small cheeses and specialty meats. While you are there pick up an assortment of fruit like grapes, pears, and local fresh berries, along with some gourmet crackers and pepper jelly. Wash the fruit but leave everything else in it's original store packaging. You will want to pack a small cutting board, a couple of sharp knives and, if legally feasible, a bottle of wine. If wine is not an option, then juice in wine glasses will create the same seductive ambiance.

Too many family picnic gatherings are bombarded with the consistently usual potato salads and coleslaws. However, no matter what salad you choose, it will require some assembly, so one is better off expending that energy by making something different. The variations of salads are endless. A quick and easy way is to create one from the ingredients you already have in your fridge and pantry. If you don't have the confidence to go this far, then blow some dust off the cookbooks you have piling up and try something you have never made before. Whatever salad you choose to prepare, pita pockets are the perfect item to serve them in. They will eliminate the need for paper plates and plastic cutlery, while adding a gourmet aura to your salad eating experience. If carbohydrates are a concern, lettuce leaves also work great as salad holders.

That brings our conversation to the next common picnic item – sandwiches. Instead of peanut butter & jelly or egg salad, why not make Italian pressed sandwiches filled with a variety of Mediterranean meats, cheeses, and complimentary flavours. This is not as hard as it sounds, as it is made in a large loaf and then cut into individual sandwiches. To ease the preparation, purchase a large Ciabatta loaf from the bakery counter. Cut it in half length-wise, and hollow out the majority of the center while keeping the shape of the outside crust in tact. You should be able to put the top back on and have it look like an untouched loaf. Fill the center with a variety of sliced meats like salami and capicolli with a complimenting cheese like provolone or shavings of parmissiano reggiano. Continue to fill the bread with gourmet olives, sundried tomatoes, capers, fresh basil and oregano, salt, fresh cracked pepper, and some extra-virgin olive oil. Put the top of the bread back on, seal it tightly with plastic wrap and refrigerate overnight with a cutting board and some heavy cans placed on top of it to press it all together combining the flavours.

Follow one simple rule to make things different and exciting: "don't settle for 'ordinary' when 'extraordinary' can be easy".

Dear Chef Dez:
I always find potato salads bland. Any suggestions?

Stephanie T.
Langley, BC

Dear Stephanie:
I am so glad you asked this question, as I always use this as a topic of discussion with my students.

Firstly, if you are boiling your potatoes, try steaming them instead. Potatoes being boiled will take on excess unnecessary water, and water has no flavour. Steaming them will help to prevent this plus they will cook faster as steam is hotter than boiling water. If you insist on boiling, then at least make sure that the water is liberally salted so the potatoes will become seasoned as they boil.

The most important thing to do however is "taste" the salad. Dressings are usually prepared separately and then mixed with the bland potatoes. People are very careful to taste their dressings in progress, and adjust the seasonings as needed, but we forget to taste the salad once it is combined. Always taste and adjust the seasonings in anything you make, just before you are serving it so that you can assess it in the same form that your guests will.

# California Rolls

*"No raw fish here! Once you get the rolling technique mastered, you will be making these for many occasions, and you will save a ton of money instead of buying them pre-made!"*

### Sushi Rice
1.5 pounds short-grain rice – approximately 3 1/3 cups
4 cups cold water
1/3 (one third) cup rice vinegar
¼ (one quarter) cup white granulated sugar
1 tablespoon salt

1. Place rice and water in a large pot, stir only once and bring to a boil over high heat. Once at a full boil, cover and simmer at the lowest temperature for 25 minutes.
2. While the rice is cooking, combine the next three ingredients in a small pot over medium heat, and cook until sugar and salt dissolve. Cool to room temperature.
3. Combine the vinegar dressing into the rice and cool mixture to room temperature.

### Fillings and Other Ingredients
1 package of 10 seaweed sheets (nori)
1 bamboo rolling mat

Traditional California rolls contain crabmeat, avocado and cucumber, but this can be substituted in part or full with a number of ingredients – be creative with tastes and colour! Here are some suggestions:

### Veggies
Cucumber, avocado, green onion, zucchini, carrot, coloured bell peppers, celery, etc.

### Seafood & other
Crabmeat, smoked or cured salmon, prawns/shrimp, egg, etc.

_Spreads_

Combinations of mayonnaise with different flavorings such as: sesame oil, wasabi, hot sauce, chili paste, hoi sin, etc…

>*HINT – when mixing mayonnaise with savory (not sweet) ingredients, add a touch of honey.

_Condiments_

Serve California rolls with pickled ginger, prepared wasabi, and a dish of soy sauce for dipping.

## California Roll Assembly

1. Set up your work station with a bamboo rolling mat directly in front of you and then the following items from left to right: seaweed sheets, sushi rice, small dish of water, flavoured mayonnaise, seafood ingredients, vegetable ingredients, and a platter/tray to put your finished rolls on.
2. Place a sheet of seaweed, with the shinier side down, on your rolling mat.
3. Arrange a thin layer of rice (with moistened hands) just over half of the bottom part of the seaweed sheet – make sure to cover evenly and to all edges and corners.
4. Spread a thin line of flavored mayonnaise horizontally across the rice and lay your seafood and vegetables fillings (3 or 4) along this line (place firmer fillings on top).
5. While lifting the mat with your thumbs, use your fingers to hold the fillings in place. The bottom edge of the seaweed being lifted should come together with the top edge of where the rice ends.
6. Compress and shape the roll with the rolling mat, leaving about an inch of seaweed open, and using your thumb – moisten this open end with water – and roll it up completely to seal the roll.
7. Finish making all 10 rolls before doing any cutting.
8. Gently cut each roll into eight even pieces, and place up the side that looks better in order for great overall presentation.

_Makes 80 pieces_

# Corn, Date, and Goat Cheese Salad

**Full colour photo available at www.chefdez.com**

*"Contrasting flavours at their finest. Loose dates in a bag or container are easier to prepare than from a brick of dates."*

2 - 341ml cans whole kernel corn, drained well
1 red bell pepper, diced small
1 & 1/3 packed cups of loose dates, finely chopped
2 large jalapeno peppers, diced small, seeds and inner membrane removed
½ (one half) cup finely chopped red onion
2 garlic cloves, crushed
¼ (one quarter) cup extra virgin olive oil
¼ (one quarter) cup balsamic vinegar
Salt & pepper to taste
Enough mixed greens for 6-8 people
200g soft unripened goat cheese

1. Mix together the corn, bell pepper, dates, jalapenos, red onion, garlic, olive oil, balsamic, salt & pepper.
2. Make individual mounds of greens for each person.
3. Top equally with the corn mixture from step one, and then the crumbled goat cheese.

*Makes 6 to 8 portions*

# Greek Tabbouleh Salad

*"My Greek version of this traditionally Middle Eastern bulgur wheat based salad"*

2 cups bulgur wheat
5 cups water
2 tsp salt
3 large garlic cloves, chopped

1. Place the bulgur in a bowl large enough to accommodate all the ingredients above. Combine the water, salt, and garlic in a small pot and bring to a boil.
2. Pour the boiling water mixture over the bulgur, cover and let sit for 30 minutes.
3. Drain the bulgur through a wire mesh sieve and place the drained bulgur/garlic in a large bowl.
4. Add the following ingredients, stir thoroughly to combine and serve immediately or refrigerate to serve later.

2 long English cucumbers, diced small
4 large Roma tomatoes, diced small
1 small yellow bell pepper, diced small
1 medium red onion, diced small
2 cups whole kalamata olives
½ (one half) cup oil packed sundried tomatoes, drained and diced small
¼ (one quarter) cup drained capers
250g feta cheese, crumbled
1 tbsp dried oregano leaves
1 tbsp dried basil leaves
½ (one half) cup extra virgin olive oil
¼ (one quarter) cup balsamic vinegar
¼ (one quarter) cup lemon juice
2 tbsp sugar
Salt & pepper to season, optional

*Makes 16 cups of salad*

# Grilled Potato Salad

*"Take a step outside of the ordinary potato salad with this grilled version. Tons of complex flavour! A great way to celebrate BC nugget potatoes."*

## Dressing

1 cup mayonnaise
1 cup sour cream
¼ (one quarter) cup liquid honey
3 tbsp apple cider vinegar
1 tbsp dried dill
2 tsp Dijon mustard
1 tsp seasoning salt
½ (one half) tsp fresh ground black pepper
½ (one half) tsp celery salt
¼ (one quarter) tsp sambal oelek

## Salad Ingredients

1.5kg BC nugget potatoes (red or white skin) *(see variation below)
2 large red bell peppers
3 tbsp olive oil
1 bunch green onions
1 large red onion, sliced into thick slices
Salt & Pepper

1.  Mix dressing ingredients thoroughly together and refrigerate.
2.  Preheat BBQ over high heat.
3.  Cut peppers into large pieces and toss with 1 tablespoon of the olive oil. Grill over high heat until charred on both sides and then place in a sealed bowl or paper bag – this will create a steaming environment that will help to loosen the skins on the pepper pieces.
4.  Toss the green onions in the residual oil from doing the red peppers and grill over high heat until slightly charred. Remove from grill and set aside.
5.  Toss the red onion slices in 1 tablespoon of the olive oil and grill over high heat until caramelized on both sides. Remove from grill and set aside.

6. Toss the potatoes with the remaining 1 tablespoon of olive oil and season with salt & pepper. Grill the potatoes whole over medium to medium-low heat until browned on all sides and cooked through, approximately 12 to 20 minutes (depending on their size). Remove from grill and set aside.

7. Peel the loosened skins from the bell peppers and discard the removed skins

8. Cut the peppers, green onions, and red onions into small pieces.

9. Cut the smallest potatoes in half, and the larger ones into quarters to make consistent bite-sized pieces.

10. Gently toss all of the cut salad ingredients with the dressing and serve immediately. If serving it later, it is important to chill the salad ingredients first before mixing with the dressing to ensure the complete salad stays chilled and keep it out of the bacteria danger zone. Remember to always follow the rule: keep cold foods cold, and keep hot foods hot.

*Makes approximately 8 side dish portions*

**VARIATION** – If baby nugget potatoes are not available, you can use 1.5kg normal red skinned potatoes, but buy them as small as possible and you will need to steam them whole for approximately 15 minutes (until half cooked) before grilling them. After grilling and when they have cooled, cut them as follows: Cut the potatoes in half. Then with each half in half (into quarter potatoes) with the skin side down. Then continue to cut the quarters (again, skin side down) into bite-size chunks. Cutting them with the skin side down will help to keep the skin on these larger potatoes.

# Homemade Muesli

**Full colour photo available at www.chefdez.com**
Recipe created by Katherine Desormeaux (Mrs. Chef Dez)
*"Use this as a yogurt or dessert topping or try it in a yogurt and fruit parfait for dessert or brunch"*

2 cups large flake oats
1 cup bran flakes cereal
1 cup slivered almonds
1 cup sweetened coconut

½ (one half) cup wheat germ

¼ (one quarter) cup sesame seeds

3 tbsp ground flax seed

1 tsp cinnamon

½ (one half) tsp salt

¼ (one quarter) cup Splenda granulated sweetener or liquid honey

½ (one half) cup canola oil

1. Preheat oven to 400 degrees.
2. Combine and mix all of the dry ingredients (including the Splenda, if that is the sweetener of your choice). If you are using honey whisk it together with the oil.
3. Drizzle the oil, or oil mixture, over the dry ingredients a little at a time stirring well between additions.
4. Spread the mixture onto a jellyroll pan or two cookie sheets. Bake stirring every 5 minutes until browned (approximately 15 minutes). Watch it closely to avoid burning.
5. Store in an airtight container.

Suggestions: Substitute sunflower seeds for the sesame seeds. Add raisins or your favourite dried fruit, after baking. Substitute your favourite kind of nuts for the almonds.

*Makes 8 cups*

# Lavender Lemonade

**Recipe created by Limbert Mountain Farm www.limbertmountainfarm.com**
*"This is our favorite lemonade and we make it for every picnic"*

8 cups water

1 heaping tbsp lavender florets (flowers, fresh or dried)

Juice of 2 lemons, approximately one half cup

½ (one half) cup sugar

1. Boil the water and remove from the heat. Add the lavender florets and steep at least 8 to 10 minutes (we actually make this the day before and leave the lavender florets in the water overnight to chill). Strain the florets out of the water and discard.

2. Transfer the water into a jar or pitcher. Add the lemon juice and sugar and mix thoroughly until the sugar has dissolved. Chill and serve each glass with a slice of lemon.

*Makes approximately 2 liters*

# Spicy Fennel Nuts

**Full colour photo available at www.chefdez.com**

*"The anise aroma and flavour from the fennel seeds make these nuts a very inviting snack. If you don't have a mortal & pestle to grind the fennel seeds, a food processor or spice grinder can be used instead."*

4 tsp fennel seeds
6 tbsp Splenda granulated sweetener
1½ (one and one half) tsp salt
1 tsp cinnamon
1 tsp cayenne pepper
1 egg white
2 cups pecan halves
1 cup whole almonds

1. Preheat oven to 300 degrees.
2. Grind the fennel seeds in a mortal & pestle until mostly ground – they do not need to be completely ground into a fine powder.
3. Combine the ground fennel seeds with the Splenda, salt, cinnamon and cayenne in a small bowl and set aside.
4. Whip the egg white to moist peaks in a large bowl.
5. Fold the spice mixture into the whipped egg white until thoroughly combined.
6. Add the pecans and almonds and gently mix together until the nuts are thoroughly coated, and then spread evenly over a large baking sheet.

7.  Bake for 25 minutes. Halfway through the baking time, use a metal flipper to separate the nuts from the pan and redistribute the nuts.

8.  Cool the cooked nut mixture on the pan until they are room temperature – the nuts will crisp up as they cool on the pan. Serve immediately or store in an air-tight container.

*Makes 3 cups*

# 3

## Remembering Mom and Her Cooking

Mother's Day is not only a day to spend time with your mom, grandmother, or wife, but also to remember and reminisce. As a child, my Mom was the biggest influence on my life and upbringing. Being a single parent of four children for many years, she persevered through many of life's obstacles to ensure a suitable developmental environment for all of us. There are many examples of her dedication to motherhood, but the fire of culinary aspirations that she fueled within me is something that I am forever grateful for.

Ever since I can remember, she was always there to offer me a spot beside her in the kitchen. While other boys my age were involved in various sports activities, my idea of a team was right there in our home. Still to this day, I can almost hear the scuffing of the old wooden footstool as I dragged it across the floor. There I would stand upon the flour-dusted crevices as she secured my apron readying me for our next culinary adventure.

Many of our kitchen conversations were a journey back in time. Descriptive adventures of what life was like when she was a child were what I loved the most. Her parents migrated to Canada from Germany in the early 1930's and they worked the land as farmers in Saskatchewan. Stories of the brutally cold winters and how most of their meals came from their crops and the pigs that they raised always kept me captivated.

As a child, she too was always by her mom's side in the kitchen. It was there that she gained the culinary skills that were passed on to me. Many of the meals that I was exposed to as a child were influenced by not only her German heritage, but also by the underprivileged lifestyle of fortuneless farmers. Creative simplicity was always the focus as we transformed everyday ingredients into something incredible. Some of the most memorable foods for me that stimulate thoughts of my childhood are rice pudding, cherry soup, and sugared milk bread slices.

'The way to a man's heart is through his stomach', but it is also the way to many great memories. Thank you Mom for the laughter, the tears, the guidance, and the years. You are always on my mind.

> Dear Chef Dez:
> I want to do something special for my wife on Mother's day. We usually go out for brunch every year, but this time I want to do something at home. Do you have any suggestions?
>
> James F.
> Abbotsford, BC

> Dear James:
> How about you and the kids prepare breakfast in bed for her? With a few extras and thoughtful ideas, breakfast in bed can be very special and meaningful. Here a few examples of what you can add to the breakfast tray along with her favorite breakfast: a cloth napkin, candles, small vase with a flower, her favorite section of the newspaper, a hand written note tied with a ribbon, a side of toast cut into heart shapes, and all the extras like coffee, tea, juice, and ice water. Most importantly, don't forget to garnish her breakfast. Mint leaves with slices of colourful fruit work very well or also add a sprinkle of cinnamon and icing sugar if appropriate. If serving juice, it can also be beautifully garnished with a slice of orange on the rim of a wine glass and frozen cranberries as ice cubes.

# Apple & Cinnamon Topped Pancakes

**Full colour photo available at www.chefdez.com**

*"Get the kids to peel the apples, measure the dry ingredients, and make homemade butter – see this chapter for the recipe"*

### Topping

2 tablespoons butter
2 apples, peeled, cored, & sliced thin
½ (one half) cup dark brown sugar
1 teaspoon cinnamon
Pinch of salt

1. Melt the butter in a non-stick pan over medium heat
2. Stir in all of the other ingredients.
3. Cook until the apples are soft and the liquid is syrupy.

### Pancakes

1 ¾ (one and three quarters) cups flour
¼ (one quarter) cup sugar
2 teaspoons baking powder
½ (one half) teaspoon salt
½ (one half) teaspoon cinnamon
Pinch ground nutmeg
Pinch ground cloves
2 eggs, beaten
¼ (one quarter) cup melted butter
1 ¼ (one and one quarter) cups milk

Whipped cream and mint leaves for garnish, optional

1. Combine all of the dry ingredients in a large mixing bowl.
2. In a separate smaller bowl, combine the wet ingredients.
3. Preheat a non-stick pan or griddle over medium heat.
4. Pour the wet ingredients into the dry ingredients and mix until just combined – DO NOT OVERMIX.

5.  With a large ladle, pour a portion of the batter onto the hot pan. Once bubbles form and start to pop on the surface of the pancakes, flip over to cook the other side until golden brown.
6.  Serve warm with a pat of homemade butter and the cooked apple & cinnamon topping.
7.  Garnish with the optional whipped cream and mint leaves, if desired.

*Makes 4 large portions.*

# Black Forest Tiramisu

**Full colour photo available at www.chefdez.com**
**Recipe created by Katherine Desormeaux (Mrs. Chef Dez)**
*"I created this recipe for, my sister, Tracey's Birthday using Splenda. You can substitute sugar for the sweetener. It is perfect for any chocolate lover and makes a showy dessert when layered into your prettiest wine glasses."*

9 squares of semi sweet bakers chocolate
1/3 (one third) cup whipping cream
1 - 8 ounce package spreadable cream cheese
½ (one half) cup Splenda granulated sweetener (or sugar)
1 tsp vanilla

1 ½ (one and one half) cups whipping cream
1 ½ (one and one half) tsp skim milk powder
1 ½ (one and one half) tsp vanilla
1/3 (one third) cup Splenda granulated sweetener (or icing sugar)

1 can cherry pie filling

1 package chocolate wafer cookies
¼ (one quarter) cup cold, strong coffee
¼ (one quarter) cup orange flavoured brandy

1. Cut 8 of the chocolate squares into small pieces (reserving the 9th one for garnish). Put the chocolate and ¼ (one quarter) cup of heavy cream into a double boiler over low heat and stir until smooth. Remove from heat.
2. Cream room temperature cream cheese, ½ (one half) cup Splenda and 1 tsp vanilla together. Pour in the warm chocolate mixture and beat until smooth.
3. Put the 1 ½ (one and one half) cups of heavy cream in the bowl of a mixer with the skim milk powder (this will keep the cream from separating if you don't serve this right away). Whip, adding the vanilla and the Splenda approximately half way through the whipping process.
4. In a separate small bowl, stir together coffee and orange brandy and set aside.
5. In large wine glasses or parfait glasses drop one tbsp of the chocolate mixture and smooth to the bottom of cup. Dip one wafer cookie briefly into the coffee/brandy mixture and place on top of chocolate. Press down slightly. Repeat with as many cookies as necessary to cover the chocolate layer (some overlapping is OK). Add a layer of whipped cream and a layer of cherry pie filling smoothing each layer to the edge of the glass. Place another layer of dipped wafers over the cherries.
6. Top with another layer of chocolate, whipped cream and cherries.
7. Garnish with a dollop of whipped cream and use a vegetable peeler to make chocolate shavings with the last square of chocolate.

*Makes 6 to 8 portions, depending upon the size of glasses used.*

# Cranberry Bread Pudding

*"A combination of both fresh and dried cranberries makes for a flavourful and more complex cranberry taste"*

1 – 454g (1 pound) French loaf
4 large eggs, beaten
1.25 cups sugar
1 tsp vanilla extract
1 tsp ground cinnamon

¼ (one quarter) tsp salt
Zest from 2 lemons, finely chopped
2 cups 10%MF cream (half and half)
2 cups milk (2%MF or 3.5%Homogenized)
¾ (three quarters) cup sweetened dried cranberries
¾ (three quarters) cup cranberries (fresh or frozen), halved
Vanilla bean ice cream, optional

1. Preheat oven to 400 degrees. Tear the French bread into approximate 1 inch to 2 inch chunks and spread evenly on a large baking sheet. Bake in the oven for 10 minutes, tossing the pieces around about halfway through. Remove from the oven and let sit while you prepare the rest of the pudding.

2. Decrease the oven temperature to 350 degrees and prepare a 9x13 baking dish by buttering it.

3. In a large bowl, combine the eggs, sugar, vanilla, cinnamon, salt, and the zest thoroughly. Whisk in the cream and milk. Add the toasted bread pieces and the dried cranberries and toss together thoroughly with your hands. Let sit for 10 minutes for the bread pieces to absorb.

4. Put one half of the custard soaked bread mixture into the prepared baking dish and top with half of the fresh/frozen halved cranberries. Add the remaining bread mixture (and scrape all liquid from the bowl) to the dish and top with the remaining fresh/frozen halved cranberries. Bake for approximately 1 hour until the top browns and puffs up. Also an inserted butter knife should come out clean.

5. Let sit for at least 10 to 15 minutes before serving warm with vanilla bean ice cream.

*Makes 10 to 12 portions*

# Fat Free Cheesecake Bites

*"If you love eating cheesecake, but are concerned with the amount of fat, calories, and cholesterol that traditional cheesecake offers, then this may be the solution. Pureeing low fat cottage cheese with lemon juice and sweetener, gives it the feel of cream cheese and the taste of cheesecake. The graham wafer pieces replace the butter laden crust that usually accompanies cheesecake. Even eating 6 of these tasty morsels is still only 96 calories and less than 2g of fat.*

1 cup of 1% cottage cheese
3 tbsp Splenda granulated sweetener
1 tbsp fresh lemon juice
1 tsp finely chopped lemon zest
½ (one half) tsp vanilla
6 graham wafers, each broken into 4 equal pieces
Whole small berries, or thinly sliced strawberries, for garnish

1.  Add all of the ingredients, except for the graham wafers and berries, into a food processor.
2.  Puree on high speed for approximately 30 seconds. Scrape down the sides and process on high speed for another 30 seconds to 1 minute, or until the mixture is smooth.
3.  Chill in the refrigerator for 2 or more hours.
4.  Top each of the wafer pieces with 2 teaspoons of the cheese mixture and a small berry or strawberry slice.

*Makes 24*

*Each cheesecake bite has approximately 16 calories, 1.5g protein, 0.3g fat, and no trans fats*

# Garlic Roasted Crab

*"A great way to cook live crab – better than boiling them whole"*

2 live crabs
1 head of garlic, chopped
½ (one half) cup butter
½ (one half) cup white wine
Juice of 1 - 2 lemons
Sprinkle of sugar
Salt & Pepper

1. Preheat oven to 400 degrees.
2. Kill crabs by knocking them upside down on the head to stun them, holding all legs on one side with one hand, then rip the shell off (in the opposite direction of the hand holding the legs) – immediately chop the body in half. Clean the crab by removing the feathery gills, innards, apron, etc. Rinse with water and chop into leg segments.
3. Place crab pieces in one or two roasting pans. Add the garlic, butter, wine, lemon juice, sugar, and season with salt & pepper.
4. Seal the pans with tin foil and roast for 20 minutes.
5. Remove the foil and serve crab pieces hot with some of the broth.

# Homemade Sauerkraut

*"A recipe from my German Grandmother. My Mom's favourite when she was a child. Thank you for sharing this with me Mom."*

2 pounds green cabbage (approximate one half medium sized head of cabbage)
1 ½ (one and one half) tbsp salt

1. Wash, core, and finely shred the cabbage.
2. Place the cabbage in a large bowl. Sprinkle with the salt and toss thoroughly to combine.
3. Let stand for approximately two hours to wilt slightly.

4. Pack the cabbage tightly into canning jars, leaving about ½ inch space from the top.

5. Fill the jars of cabbage with cold water. Put the lids on the jars and screw them on snuggly – but not tight! Place the jars on a pan to catch any brine that overflows during fermentation.

6. Store in a cool dark place (55 to 60 degrees Fahrenheit) to ferment for 6 to 8 weeks – it is important to ensure the temperature is not too hot or too cold, otherwise the cabbage will spoil. Do not eat if spoiled.

7. It is important to check the cabbage daily to ensure that it is kept covered with brine, and remove any scum that forms. To make extra brine dissolve 1 tbsp salt into 2 cups water, and add to cabbage as necessary.

8. After the 6 to 8 week curing process, store the sauerkraut in the refrigerator before using within a couple of weeks.

9. For best results, sauté drained sauerkraut with butter and red onions!

# Homemade Syrup

*"A very quick and easy solution for when you have run out of syrup and the pancake ingredients are already assembled! My Mother-in-Law used to make this for my wife when she was a child. Thank you for sharing this with me Bonnie!"*

1 cup dark brown sugar
1 cup white sugar
1 cup water
½ to 1 tsp maple extract
Pinch of salt

1. Combine all ingredients in a small pot. Heat over medium-low heat to dissolve the sugars, but do not let it boil.

2. Serve immediately or cool and serve and room temperature. Keep it over low heat to reduce out more of the water to make it thicker.

# Monte Cristo Bread Pudding

*"The classic Monte Cristo Sandwich, but prepared like a bread pudding in an individual baking dish"*

2 thick slices of sandwich bread
50g ham, diced small
40g Gruyere or Gouda cheese, grated
1 egg
1/3 (one third) cup milk
1 tbsp finely chopped onion
¼ (one quarter) tsp Worcestershire sauce
1/8 (one eighth) tsp dry mustard
1/8 (one eighth) tsp salt
Pinch of pepper
1 to 2 drops Tabasco sauce
Finely chopped fresh parsley for garnish, optional

1. Cube 1 slice of the bread into approximately ½ (one half) inch cubes and place them in the bottom of a 2-cup oven-proof dish.
2. Top with the ham, then the other 20g of cheese, and the second slice of bread, cubed.
3. In a small bowl, mix thoroughly together the egg, milk, onion, Worcestershire, mustard, salt, pepper, and Tabasco, and pour over the bread, ham, and cheese in the dish.
4. Top with the second 20g of grated cheese. Cover and refrigerate overnight for the bread to soak up the egg mixture.
5. Preheat oven to 350 degrees.
6. Remove the cover from the dishes and bake uncovered for approximately 35 to 45 minutes until the egg has cooked through and the cheese has browned. Let stand for 5 minutes, garnish with parsley and serve.

*Makes 1 individual portion*

*\*Helpful Tip: If mixing the egg mixture for more than one recipe (one portion) do not add the onion to the egg mixture. Instead add the 1 tbsp chopped onion directly onto the top layer of cubed bread for each portion and pour the egg mixture over top. This will ensure that each portion gets the right amount of onion.*

# Pralines with Sweet Biscuits & Rum Flambéed Bananas

**Full colour photo available at www.chefdez.com**

*"Prepare the bananas last to serve them warm from the pan"*

## Pralines Ingredients
½ (one half) cup butter
½ (one half) cup dark brown sugar
½ (one half) cup white sugar
¼ (one quarter) cup whipping cream
¼ (one quarter) tsp salt
1 ½ (one and one half) cups pecans

## Sweet Biscuits Ingredients
2 ¼ (two and one quarter) cups flour
3 tbsp sugar
1 ½ (one and one half) tbsp baking powder
½ (one half) tsp salt
6 tbsp cold or frozen butter
¾ (three quarters) cup sour cream
6 tbsp milk or water

## Flambéed Bananas Ingredients
¼ (one quarter) cup butter
¼ (one quarter) cup dark brown sugar
Pinch of salt
3 bananas, not overly ripe
2 – 3 tbsp rum

## Other Ingredients
Vanilla ice cream
Fresh mint leaves

## Pralines

1. Prepare a baking sheet by lining it with parchment paper and spray with baking spray.
2. Add all of the Praline ingredients except for the pecans to a heavy bottomed pot. Heat over medium heat until butter has melted.
3. Stir in the pecans and bring to a boil. Once boiling, reduce heat to medium-low and cook for approximately 15 – 20 minutes, stirring occasionally until the sugar cooks to "Hard Ball Stage" (250-260 degrees F). Test by dropping a bit of hot sugar into a saucer of cold water: the sugar should be just pliable enough for you to be able to shape it into a firm ball of candy, and once thoroughly cooled, it should retain its shape. **Handle the hot sugar with extreme care, as it is extremely hot and will stick and burn skin instantly!**
4. With a silicone scraper, remove all of the cooked praline and spread onto the prepared baking sheet. Let cool in the refrigerator or freezer until solid. Break into pieces as desired.

## Sweet Biscuits

1. Preheat the oven to 450 degrees, and spray a baking sheet with baking spray.
2. In a mixing bowl, combine the flour, sugar, baking powder, and salt.
3. With a coarse grater, grate the cold butter into the dry ingredients and gently toss together to mix/coat the butter pieces.
4. In a separate small bowl, stir the sour cream and milk together.
5. Pour the sour cream/milk mixture into the dry ingredients and gently start to mix together until both parts start coming together. Empty the contents onto the counter and work the dough gently until it almost fully comes together and is approximate shape of a 4 x 6 rectangle. **Be careful not to overwork the dough, as overworking will make a tough biscuit.**
6. With a sharp knife cut the dough into 6 biscuits, place them on the prepared baking sheet and bake for approximately 10-12 minutes until cooked and slightly golden.

<u>Flambéed Bananas</u>

1.  Add the butter, sugar, and salt to a non-stick pan over medium heat.
2.  Cut the bananas in half lengthwise and remove/discard the peels. Cut the banana halves crosswise into 3 pieces each. This will make 18 pieces.
3.  Once the butter has melted, and the banana pieces and stir to coat. Once hot, carefully add the rum and carefully ignite with a long match or grill lighter. Shake the pan until the flames subside.
4.  Cook the bananas until heated through and the sauce has thickened a bit, approximately 2 – 3 minutes.
5.  Remove from heat.

<u>Assembly</u>

For each portion, cut 1 biscuit in half and place the bottom half on a plate. Top with vanilla ice cream, sprinkled pralines, & 3 banana pieces. Then place on the top half of the biscuit, garnish with sauce from the bananas, a mint leaf, and serve immediately.

*Makes 6 portions*

# 4
## *Food for Dad on Father's Day*

My Dad is a real meat & potatoes kind of guy, and doesn't stray from this beaten path very often. Although he appreciates good food and has a palette accepting of spiciness, he usually doesn't like anything too fancy or extraordinary. Many Dads fall into this category and thus I dedicate this column to them and the loved ones that cook for them.

Being a Dad myself, I immediately think of barbequed food when it comes to father's day. Instead of grilling up the same old cookout fare like hamburgers and hotdogs, allow me to give you some refreshing ideas to add some variety to your celebration.

A very popular recipe for beer chicken has been circulating for a while now. It involves standing a seasoned chicken over an open can of beer. Closing the lid of the barbeque will allow the chicken to roast and have the moisture of the beer baste the inside of the chicken as it evaporates from the can. This produces a very juicy and flavouful chicken and is sure to be a popular item with Dad.

Another great idea for the barbeque is corn on the cob. Most people boil cobbed corn, but how much flavour does water have? Zero. A better way is to have them steam in their own juices directly on the grates of the grill. The way to prepare this flavorful corn is very simple and provides a fantastic presentation. Remove as much of the silk as possible while keeping the husks of the corn in tact. Soak the ears or corn for at least one hour in a pot of water to help prevent them from drying out. Remove from the water and place them directly on the preheated grill of the barbeque. With the ears in tact, the cobs of corn will now steam in their own husks which will get somewhat charred, adding a smoky flavour. Depending on the temperature of your barbeque, this will take approximately 10 to 20 minutes (remember to rotate them). For the best presentation, pull back the husks but keep them attached. An optional mixture of softened butter seasoned with salt, pepper, and chili powder will add an extra kick of flavour and colour.

One of my most favorite barbeque side dishes is grilled red onion. With the help of a marinade, slices of this sweet onion variety get caramelized and sugary on the grill. A simple marinade of soy sauce and liquid honey will work wonders for you. Simply slice the red onions into 1 to 2 cm thick slices and insert two skewers per slice to keep them from falling apart into onion 'rings'. Mix the marinade and soak the slices for one to twelve hours, turning occasionally. Preheat the barbeque and grill on each side until caramelized. Season with salt & freshly cracked pepper and serve.

These are just a few of the endless dishes that you can accomplish for a fantastic father's day meal. There are many unique and tasty recipes available to you on the internet and at the library, and one should always take advantage of these resources.

Dear Chef Dez:
I love barbequed chicken with the skin on, however it always seems to get burned on the outside well before the center gets cooked. I know many people cook skinless chicken pieces and they have no problem, but I enjoy having the skin on. However, the fat from the skin promotes flare-ups, and thus gets burned. How can I avoid this without losing my enjoyment of having the skin?

Tracey S.
Abbotsford, BC

Dear Tracey:
There are two ways you can go about preventing this. One way is to use a combination of cooking methods between the oven and the barbeque. Starting the cooking process of the chicken in your oven will cook much of the fat from the skin before it even hits the grill. Lay seasoned chicken pieces in a baking dish and cook halfway through. Then transfer them to a preheated grill to get the flame-broiled taste and to finish the cooking process. Barbeque sauce is best added just before the chicken is cooked on the barbeque.

CHEF DEZ

*If this seems like too much effort, the other way is to use lower heat on the barbeque and place the chicken pieces on an upper rack (if equipped). This will take more time than the first option, however by doing all the grilling outside, your home will stay that much cooler.*

# BBQ Beef Po' Boy Sandwich

*"A sandwich extravaganza; rumors say "Po'Boys" began as a five cent lunch for, what else, poor boys. Served on crusty French bread loaves, Po'Boys now come in all types and sizes... and this one is extremely large – 4 to 8 portions, depending on appetite!"*

## BBQ Sauce Ingredients
¾ (three quarters) cup ketchup
¼ (one quarter) cup brown sugar
2 garlic cloves, crushed
2 tbsp white vinegar
1 tbsp lemon juice
2 tsp canola oil
½ (one half) tsp cinnamon
½ (one half) tsp salt
½ (one half) tsp pepper
Dash of ground cloves

## Other Ingredients
800g beef flank steak
2 large red bell peppers
1 red onion, sliced thick
2 tsp canola oil
1 large tomato, sliced thick
200-300g Monterey Jack cheese, sliced
¼ (one quarter) cup butter, room temp.
2 garlic cloves, crushed
1 large French bread

Mayonnaise
Dijon mustard
Salt & pepper
Leaf lettuce

1. Mix ingredients for the BBQ sauce.
2. Place the flank steak in a closeable plastic bag with the BBQ sauce and let sit in the refrigerator for a minimum of 1 hour.
3. Cut the sides off the bell peppers. Toss these and the red onion slices with the canola oil.
4. Preheat BBQ grill. Remove the flank steak from the BBQ sauce. Pour the BBQ sauce into a small pot ad bring to a constant boil for a minimum of 1 to 2 minutes. Set aside.
5. Cook the flank steak for approximately 5 – 7 minutes per side, with the lid open, over medium-high heat for medium-rare to medium doneness – depending on the thickness of the steak. At the same time grill the red pepper sides and red onion slices until cooked.
6. Remove the steak and let it rest for 2 – 3 minutes before slicing to help retain the juiciness of the meat. Once the steak has rested, slice the steak across the grain into thin strips, just before assembling the sandwich to help retain the heat.
7. Remove the red onions and set aside.
8. Remove the red peppers and place in an airtight bowl for a few minutes. This will help make removing the skins easier.
9. Mix the butter with the crushed garlic and set aside.
10. Cut the French loaf in half, lengthwise.
11. Spread the garlic butter on the insides of both halves of the bread.
12. Spread desired amount of mayonnaise on the top half, and spread desired amount of Dijon mustard on the bottom half.
13. Assemble as follows starting on the bottom half of the loaf: grilled red onions, sliced beef, BBQ sauce, peeled bell peppers, cheese, tomatoes, salt & pepper, lettuce leafs, and the top half of the loaf.
14. Insert long skewers into each portion of the sandwich prior to cutting to assist in keeping the sandwich together once cut.

# Cajun Pan-Fried Walleye

*"An inspiration from my Father-in-Law, Ron. The center of attention of shore lunch on Lake of the Woods is always pan-fried walleye – this is my Cajun version of it."*

4 to 6 small walleye filets, or other favorite fish
½ (one half) cup flour
1 egg
2 tbsp milk
¼ (one quarter) cup olive oil
Small chopped red pepper and chopped parsley for garnish

*Breading*
12 stoned wheat crackers
2 tbsp paprika
2 tsp cayenne pepper
1 tsp salt
¼ (one quarter) tsp black pepper

1. Prepare breading by processing the five ingredients in a food processor on high speed for approximately 30 seconds.
2. Gently rinse the filets under running water and drain.
3. Put the flour on a plate.
4. Beat the egg and milk together in a small bowl.
5. Bread the filets as follows:
    1. Dredge each filet in the flour until well coated.
    2. Dip in the egg wash.
    3. Dredge each filet in the breading and set aside on a clean plate.
6. Heat the olive oil in a heavy-bottomed pan over medium heat.
7. Pan-fry the filets for approximately 2 to 3 minutes on each side.
8. Set the filets on clean paper towel for a few seconds to drain.
9. Serve warm and garnish the plates with the diced red pepper, chopped parsley, and a sprinkle of paprika.

*Makes 4 to 6 portions*

# Cajun Pork Tenderloin

**Full colour photo available at www.chefdez.com**

*"The tenderloin is brined in salt water to help keep it juicy and flavourful"*

4 cups cold water
¼ (one quarter) cup table salt
3 or 4 - 1 lb pork tenderloins
½ (one half) cup paprika
4 tsp ground black pepper
4 tsp ground dried oregano
1 tsp salt
1 - 2 tsp cayenne pepper

*Garlic Butter (mix together)*
½ (one half) cup melted butter
2 garlic cloves, crushed
2 tsp finely chopped parsley

1. Dissolve the ¼ (one quarter) cup table salt in the 4 cups of water. Add the tenderloin, and brine for one hour in the refrigerator.
2. Preheat oven to 400 degrees.
3. Remove the tenderloin and pat dry. Mix the next five ingredients in a small bowl to make a dry rub. Apply this rub to all areas of the tenderloin.
4. Roast the tenderloin in the oven for 20 –25 minutes. Let sit for 5 – 10 minutes before slicing. Drizzle with garlic butter when serving.

*Makes 10-12 servings*

# Chipotle Mayonnaise

*"Canned chipotle peppers from the Mexican foods section of your grocery store are an easy way to spice up mayonnaise for an incredible dipping sauce or sandwich spread"*

½ (one half) cup mayonnaise
1 or 2 canned chipotle peppers

1.  Add the ingredients to a food processor – start with 1 chipotle pepper.
2.  Puree until smooth. Taste and add an additional pepper if you want it spicier (then process again).
3.  Serve immediately as a dipping sauce or sandwich spread, or keep chilled in the refrigerator.

*Makes just over one half cup*

# Grilled Meat Jambalaya

*"Grilling the meat brings extra flavor to this classic Mardi Gras dish"*

2 tsp canola oil
1 medium onion, diced small
1 medium red bell pepper, diced small
1 celery stalk, diced small
6 garlic cloves, minced
½ (one half) tsp salt
1 ½ (one and one half) cups long grain white rice
1 - 284ml can condensed chicken broth
1 - 240ml bottle clam juice
1 – 398ml can diced tomatoes, not drained
1 tsp dried thyme leaves
2 bay leaves
2 tsp sugar
1 tsp ground cayenne pepper
4 boneless skinless chicken thighs

canola oil
salt & pepper
200g chorizo sausage
454g (1 pound) cooked large shrimp
fresh parsley, chopped for garnish

1. Heat a heavy bottomed pot over medium heat.
2. Add the oil and then the onion, bell pepper, celery, garlic, and salt. Stir to combine and cook until soft, approximately 2 – 3 minutes stirring occasionally.
3. Add the rice, condensed broth, clam juice, tomatoes, thyme, bay leaves, sugar, and cayenne. Stir to combine. Turn the heat to high and bring to a boil.
4. Cover, reduce the heat to low, and simmer for 20 minutes.
5. Keep the pot covered, remove from the heat and let stand for 5 minutes.
6. **While the rice mixture is cooking, prepare and grill the chicken as sausage as follows:**
7. Oil the chicken thighs and season with salt and pepper. Grill for approximately 7 – 8 minutes per side over medium high heat until cooked through. Grill the whole sausages over lower heat until the outside is slightly charred. Chorizo sausages are usually pre-cooked when you buy them (check with your deli), so this is just to get more of a flame-licked smoky flavour to them.
8. Remove the chicken and sausage from the grill and let stand a few minutes. Cut the chicken and sausage into "bite-sized" pieces.
9. Remove the bay leaves from the rice mixture and stir in the grilled meats. Then stir in the cooked shrimp and serve immediately, garnished with the chopped parsley. (Since the shrimp is already cooked it is added last to just warm them through without overcooking them. Overcooked shrimp have a rubber-like texture.)

*Makes 4 to 6 servings.*

# Mozza Stuffed Hamburgers

*"Loaded with flavour, these burgers will be the hit at your next bar-be-que! See the Blueberry Chapter in this book for a Blueberry version of these great burgers."*

1 kg lean ground beef

8 garlic cloves, crushed

1 egg

2/3 (two thirds) cup cornflake crumbs

½ (one half) cup minced onion

½ (one half) cup oil packed sundried tomatoes, drained & chopped

¼ (one quarter) cup berry jam

1 tbsp salt

1 tbsp dried basil leaves

2 tsp sambal oelek

1 tsp dried thyme leaves

1 tsp chilli powder

1 tsp pepper

100g mozzarella cheese, cut into 8 small chunks

1. Mix all of the ingredients together (except for the mozzarella) in a large bowl.
2. Preheat your cooking surface; pan, grill, griddle, etc.
3. Portion the hamburger mixture into eight equal sized balls.
4. Flatten each ball in your hand and encase a chunk of mozzarella in the middle by shaping it into a large patty, by wrapping the meat around the cheese.
5. Over a medium heat/flame, cook the patties until thoroughly cooked through, approximately 8 to 12 minutes per side.

*Ground hamburger patties must be completely cooked through to be safely consumed.

*Makes 8 large patties*

# My Dad's Famous Chipotle Spaghetti Sauce

**Full colour photo available at www.chefdez.com**
**Recipe created by Robert Desormeaux (Dez Senior)**

*"I had to include this recipe in my book! My Dad means the world to me, and he always teases me about the rave reviews he gets about this sauce."*

2 pounds lean ground beef
1 medium/large onion
1 medium carrot
1 stalk celery
4 garlic cloves
1 medium green bell pepper
2 – small cans sliced mushrooms, drained
1 – 796ml can diced tomatoes
1 – 700ml jar pasta sauce
1 package dry pasta sauce seasoning mix
1 tbsp hot dry mustard
1 tsp Worcestershire
1 tsp pepper
½ (one half) tsp chipotle seasoning, or to taste *see note below

1.  Brown the beef in a large pan/pot over medium heat.
2.  Pulse the onion, carrot, celery, garlic and green pepper in a food processor until minced. Add this to the cooked beef and continue to cook until these vegetables have softened.
3.  Add the remaining ingredients and simmer for a minimum of 1 to 3 hours or until desired consistency has been reached. Season to taste with salt and a bit of sugar. Serve immediately with your choice of pasta.

*Note: If you cannot find dry chipotle seasoning, then buy a can of chipotle peppers and use one half a pepper minced instead (or to taste).

# No-Cook BBQ Sauce

*"Great for the kids to make for Dad on Father's day"*

½ (one half) cup ketchup
1 tablespoon molasses
1 teaspoon white vinegar
½ (one half) teaspoon chili powder
½ (one half) teaspoon Worcestershire sauce
½ (one half) teaspoon hot sauce **or** 2 drops Tabasco sauce
Pinch of salt
Sprinkle of cinnamon
Couple drops of liquid smoke, optional

1. Mix together and keep refrigerated.


# Saucy Little Meat Loaves

**Full colour photo available at www.chefdez.com**

*"Individual meat loaves with a zesty sauce – loaded with flavour"*

1.5 pounds (680g) lean ground beef
1 egg
½ (one half) cup quick oats
¼ (one quarter) cup minced onion
4 cloves garlic, crushed
1 tbsp dark brown sugar
1.5 tsp salt
1 tsp chili powder
1 tsp dried basil leaves
½ (one half) tsp pepper
1 – 680ml can of tomato sauce
½ (one half) cup blueberry jam or grape jelly
¼ (one quarter) cup dark brown sugar

4 tsp cornstarch
2 tsp Worcestershire sauce
1 tsp salt
Pinch of pepper

1.  Preheat oven to 400 degrees.
2.  Combine the ground beef with the egg, oats, onion, garlic, tbsp brown sugar, salt, chili powder, basil, pepper, and ½ cup of the tomato sauce. Shape into 6 ovals (loaves) in a shallow baking dish and bake for 20 minutes.
3.  Combine the remaining tomato sauce, jam/jelly, brown sugar, cornstarch, Worcestershire, salt and pepper in a bowl.
4.  At the end of the 20 minute baking time, remove the fat from the pan and pour the sauce mixture over the loaves. Bake 10 minutes longer.

*Makes 6 portions*

# 5

## Pepper: The World's Most Popular Spice

**M**any people would assume that the most used spice is "salt". However, salt is actually a mineral, not a spice. This leaves its sidekick 'pepper' in the lead for the number one position.

Peppercorns as we know them are the dried result of the 'piper nigrum' berry and have been harvested for thousands of years. In ancient times the value of this pungent spice was even elevated to the degree of being used as trading barter much like currency. The four most popular types of peppercorns that dominate our current food markets are black, white, green and pink.

**Black peppercorns** are obviously the most prevalent and also the least expensive. They are produced by harvesting the berries before they are fully ripe and drying them. The drying process is what gives them their black hard wrinkled appearance and texture. These are not only the most popular but also the most pungent of the varieties. The best flavour and aroma is obtained by freshly grinding them directly on or in the dish you are preparing. Pre-ground spices always lose their freshness and ability to season as time passes. Logically, fresher is always better.

**White peppercorns** are derived from the same type of berries that the black peppercorns come from, however they are allowed to mature before harvesting.

They are then either soaked or washed in water to remove the outer shell, which produces a white peppercorn with a milder taste. They are frequently utilized to season white sauces to ensure that the appearance of the sauce is not marred with black specs.

**Green peppercorns** are one of my ultimate favorites in sauces. These peppercorns are harvested when they are still very immature, and either dried or preserved in brine. They offer a more natural temperate flavour, and when brined are very soft and can be eaten whole. These are great for transforming ordinary gravy into a gourmet peppercorn sauce with the help of a jigger of brandy or wine. The dried green peppercorns can be rehydrated to make them pliable to accomplish this same task. They can also be mashed into a paste for different applications.

**Pink peppercorns** are not actually peppercorns in the same definition as referred to in the above-mentioned examples. They are berries that look similar to the 'piper nigrum' berry but are sweeter, milder, and more aromatic. They can ripen to even a dark red in colour before harvesting. These are great in delicately flavoured recipes and offer great presentation as well.

In light of all the choices you have, it should be apparent that pepper is nothing to sneeze at.

*Dear Chef Dez:*

*A sales clerk at a department store told me that I should buy a hand-held pepper mill instead of using a shaker. She said that pepper freshly ground from a pepper mill, is better than pepper that is purchased already ground. I guess this does make sense - is this true? If so, should I buy one of those salt mills too?*

*Gladys L.*
*Langley, BC*

*Dear Gladys:*

*This is true. Grinding pepper fresh from a mill releases the essential oils and aromatics trapped inside whole peppercorns, and the taste difference is incredible. Like other spices, once ground it is only a matter of time before it becomes stale. Salt mills on the other hand, are more for esthetic appeal. Salt minerals do not have essential oils and thus grinding them fresh will make no difference in taste. The only thing you will gain from using a salt grinder is the unique texture of the irregular shaped crystals falling on your food.*

# Nothin' But Love Indian Caesar Appy

**Full colour photo available at www.chefdez.com**

*"The spice of Indian cuisine combined with seafood and Caesar salad on crispy bits of bread makes for a very delicious appetizer! Serve with a gewürztraminer wine to offer a bit of sweetness to offset the heat of the spices on the palate."*

<u>Dressing</u>
2 tbsp lemon juice
2 tbsp ground coriander
1 tbsp Dijon mustard
1 ½ (one and one half) tsp ground turmeric
1 tsp Worcestershire sauce
2 ½ (two and one half) anchovies
3 garlic cloves
2 tsp minced fresh ginger
2 egg yolks
2 dashes of tobasco sauce
½ (one half) tsp salt
1 cup canola or vegetable oil

<u>Spice Blend</u>
2 cinnamon sticks
12 whole cloves
8 cardamom pods, with outer husks removed
2 tsp cumin seed
1 ½ (one and one half) tsp whole black peppercorns
1 tsp cayenne pepper
1 tsp ground ginger
1 tsp fennel seed
½ (one half) tsp salt

<u>Other ingredients</u>
4 or 5 naan breads, cut into 36 hand-held pieces
2 tbsp canola or vegetable oil
1 tbsp butter
3 garlic cloves, crushed

18 large prawns
54 small scallops
5 or 6 leaves of romaine lettuce, cut into bite sized pieces

1. Process all of the ingredients for the dressing, except for the canola oil, in a food processor.
2. With the food processor running at top speed, gradually and the oil in a very slow steady stream until fully incorporated. Set this dressing aside. For ease of assembly, it is best put into a squirt bottle.
3. Combine all of the ingredients in the spice blend into a spice grinder and process until completely ground and amalgamated together. Set aside.
4. Preheat oven to 450 degrees. Place the naan pieces on a large baking sheet and bake in the preheated oven for 5 minutes. Flip the pieces over and continue baking for another 5 minutes, or until completely toasted on both sides. Set aside.
5. In a large non-stick pan, add the 2 tablespoons of oil with the butter and crushed garlic. Turn the heat to medium. As soon as the butter has melted (so you don't burn the garlic), add the prawns, scallops and the spice blend from the above step number 3. Turn the heat to medium-high and cook stirring frequently for approximately 5 to 7 minutes until the prawns and scallops are just cooked through (do not overcook or they will turn rubbery).

## Assembly

1. On each piece of toasted naan, drizzle a small amount of dressing.
2. Top each with 2 or 3 pieces of romaine lettuce.
3. Drizzle another small amount of dressing onto the romaine.
4. Top 18 of the appies with the spiced prawns and the other 18 with 3 spiced scallops each.

*makes 36 appetizers*

# Peppered Cheese Bread

**Full colour photo available at www.chefdez.com**

*"A quick bread with tons of cheese and pepper flavours! For best results make sure you use old cheddar and fresh cracked black pepper."*

2 cups flour (plus more for dusting)
2 tbsp sugar
4 tsp baking powder
1 ½ (one and one half) tsp salt
1 ½ (one and one half) tsp freshly cracked pepper
1 tbsp soft green Madagascar peppercorns, drained
2 cups grated old cheddar cheese
2 eggs, beaten
1 cup milk
1 tbsp melted butter
More pepper for sprinkling

1. Preheat oven to 350 degrees and prepare a 9 inch pie plate with baking spray and then dusting it with flour.
2. In a large bowl combine the flour, sugar, baking powder, salt, and pepper. Toss in the green peppercorns and 1.5 cups of the grated cheese to thoroughly coat with the flour mixture.
3. In a separate bowl mix together the eggs, milk, and melted butter.
4. Pour the wet mixture into the dry mixture. Stir until just combined and spread the mixture into the prepared pie plate.
5. Top with the remaining one half cup cheddar and more freshly cracked pepper.
6. Bake for approximately 30 to 35 minutes until the bread is solid and the cheese has browned slightly on top.
7. Let cool in the pie plate for at least 10 minutes before trying to remove it, and then let cool thoroughly on a cooling rack.

*Makes one 9-inch round loaf*

# Pepper Steak Madagascar

**Full colour photo available at www.chefdez.com**

2 top grade Strip Loin steaks
1 ½ (one and one half) tbsp freshly cracked black peppercorns
Salt
1 tbsp oil
2/3 (two thirds) cup full bodied red wine
2 tbsp concord grape jelly (or other PREMIUM grape jelly)
1/3 - 1/2 (one third to one half) cup whipping cream
¼ (one quarter) cup concentrated beef stock (undiluted - straight from the can)
2 tbsp green Madagascar peppercorns, strained from brine
1 tbsp butter
Fresh parsley, chopped – for garnish - optional

1. Crush the black peppercorns.
2. Season steaks with salt and coat with the crushed peppercorns.
3. Heat a heavy pan over medium-high heat. Pour in oil and sear the steaks - approximately 2 minutes per side for rare (depending on thickness of steaks).
4. Remove the steaks from the pan, and cover them to keep warm.
5. Take the pan off the heat and deglaze with the merlot.
6. Turn the heat to medium and replace the pan to the burner. Add the grape jelly and cook until the wine has reduced by half, and the jelly has melted into the wine.
7. Add the cream and beef stock. Turn the heat to medium-high and reduce until the sauce has almost thickened completely.
8. Add the green peppercorns.
9. Add the steaks back to the pan just to reheat and coat with the sauce.
10. Plate the steaks with the presentation side (the side with less fat) forward.
11. Reduce the sauce further until syrupy and stir in the butter. Taste and re-season if necessary.
12. Spoon the sauce over the steaks and down the front of the presentation sides. Garnish with fresh chopped parsley, if desired.

*Makes 2 portions*

# 6

## Fresh Herbs or Dried Herbs?

Many consumers, without herb gardens of their own, will choose to purchase dried herbs more frequently than fresh due to cost and convenience. Dried herbs are suitable for certain recipe applications, however there are just as many recipes that would benefit from fresh. Consequently, other than listening to your wallet, how should one discriminate choosing between them?

Although fresh herbs seem to offer the most flavour, they are not a necessity for all recipes. Dried herbs need time and moisture to release their flavours, and therefore are adequate in dishes that require a certain amount of cooking time to allow for this re-hydration. Examples of these recipes would be ones such as pasta sauce, chili, soups, or other stewed dishes. Fresh herbs can be used in these applications, but are better suited being added at the end of the cooking process, as they can loose their potency if cooked for too long.

Many people also use dried herbs in marinades and compound butters. Compound butters are combinations of herbs, seasonings, and flavourings combined with butter to create finishing touches to certain dishes. Garlic butter, for example, is probably the most recognizable compound butter.

A large misconception with dried herbs, however, is that they last forever. They don't. There are steps one can take to inhibit their deterioration like storing them in a cool dark place, but eventually they will lose their pungency.

Typically, I would suggest replacing dried herbs every six to eight months if stored properly. I have found that the bulk foods sections at the grocery stores are the best option for doing this economically. Get in the habit of only purchasing slightly more than what you need for a recipe. This will keep your home inventory low and your recipes tasting better.

Since the moisture (water content) has been removed from dried herbs, they are more potent (per measure) than fresh herbs. This is an important consideration when changing a recipe to accommodate the herbs you have on hand. The only herb, that this rule is not applicable to, is tarragon – it is more potent (per measure) in its fresh form.

Given the choice to be stranded on a dessert island with either herb form, I would obviously pick fresh for its versatility, nutrients, and fresh flavour. However, it is important to understand that dried herbs, when used and stored correctly, can play a vital role in our kitchens.

Dear Chef Dez:
I was recently given some fresh basil and added it to a pasta sauce I was making. I didn't notice much difference in flavour than using dried basil, in fact I noticed less. Is this right?

Margarette T.
Coquitlam, BC

Dear Margarette:
This depends on how much basil you added and when you added it. Most dried herbs are more potent in the dry form as the flavour intensity is higher without water content. Therefore you would need to add a larger measurement of fresh then you would dry.

When adding delicate fresh herbs, such as basil, do it at the end of the cooking process, about 30 seconds before serving. This will guarantee that the fresh flavours of the basil will be prevalent in your dish.

CHEF DEZ

# Herbes de Provence Vinaigrette

*"A basic vinaigrette focused on the herbes de Provence flavours"*

½ (one half) cup extra virgin olive oil
½ (one half) cup white wine vinegar
1 garlic clove, crushed
1 tbsp finely chopped fresh thyme
1 tsp finely chopped fresh basil
1 tsp finely chopped fresh rosemary
½ (one half) tsp dried marjoram leaves
½ (one half) tsp dried lavender flowers
1 tsp salt
1 tsp sugar
½ (one half) tsp fresh cracked pepper

- Place all ingredients in a mixing bowl and whisk until combined ~ or ~ place all ingredients in a jar and shake until combined. Serve immediately after combining before it has a chance to separate.

*Makes just over 1 cup*

# Pastry Wrapped Herbes de Provence Camembert

**Full colour photo available at www.chefdez.com**

*"A rich appetizer that celebrates the tastes of French cuisine"*

1 egg
1 tbsp water
1 – 400g package of frozen puff pastry, thawed and kept cold
Flour
200g wheel of Camembert cheese, kept chilled, cut into 8 equal pieces
1 recipe of Herbes de Provence vinaigrette, approximately 1 cup

1. Preheat oven to 425 degrees.
2. Line a baking sheet with parchment paper, or spray with baking spray.
3. Whisk the egg and water together and set aside.
4. Cut the puff pastry into 8 equal pieces. On a lightly floured surface, roll each one into an approximate 5 inch by 5 inch square, approximately 1/8 inch thick, using just as much flour as you need to keep it from sticking to the rolling pin and counter.
5. Place 1 piece of Camembert in the center of each square of pastry and press the cheese to make an indent big enough to hold one tablespoon of vinaigrette.
6. Brush the edges of each pastry square with the reserved egg wash.
7. Shake or whisk the vinaigrette to combine and immediately put 1 tablespoon of the vinaigrette on each of the Camembert pieces. Carefully pull the sides of the pastry up and press together over the filling, ensuring to seal up all the edges as much as possible.
8. Place the pastry bundles on the prepared pan and brush the outsides with the remaining egg wash and bake for approximately 17 to 20 minutes until golden brown.
9. Plate each bundle by with another tablespoon of vinaigrette drizzled over each one, and garnish with a fresh herb of your choice (or any combination) from the herbs used in the vinaigrette.

*Makes 8 portions*

# Peach and Thyme Pork Chops

**Full colour photo available at www.chefdez.com**

*"The amount of sugar you use will depend on the sweetness of your peaches – start with one tablespoon and then add the other tablespoon at the end if needed"*

6 pork loin center chops, boneless
1 tbsp canola oil
Salt & pepper
½ (one half) cup white wine
½ (one half) cup chicken broth

5 to 6 peaches, peeled, pitted, and sliced
3 cloves of garlic, minced
2 tbsp fresh thyme leaves
1 to 2 tbsp sugar

1. Heat a large heavy bottomed pan over medium-high heat.
2. Coat the chops with oil and season both sides with salt & pepper. Sear the chops on both sides, approximately 3 to 4 minutes total.
3. Add the wine, broth, peaches, garlic, thyme and sugar to the pan and stir slightly to combine and bring to a boil.
4. Cover, turn the heat down to medium-low, and cook for 8 minutes.
5. Remove the lid, turn the chops over, and cook with no lid for another 7 minutes.
6. Remove the chops from the pan and set them aside. Increase the heat to medium-high and reduce the sauce until syrupy. Serve immediately.

*Makes 6 portions*

# Tomato & Sausage Clams

**Full colour photo available at www.chefdez.com**

*"This is one of my favourites! My version of "surf & turf". Nothing beats sitting down with a big bowl of this with a glass of wine and a big chunk of crusty bread!"*

300g mild Italian sausage
2 tbsp extra virgin olive oil
1 head (8-12 cloves) garlic, minced
1 tbsp fennel seed
2 tsp dried oregano
1 tsp dried thyme
1 – 796ml can diced tomatoes, drained
½ (one half) cup white wine
3 bay leaves
1 tsp sugar
1kg fresh live littleneck clams, scrubbed

Salt & pepper
Fresh parsley, chopped, for garnish
Fresh lemon wedges
Large crusty loaf of Italian bread

1. Squeeze sausage out of casings into a large heavy bottomed pan over medium to medium-high heat. Add the olive oil, garlic, fennel, oregano, and thyme. While pan is heating, mix together while breaking up the sausage with a wooden spoon. Cook for approximately 4 – 6 minutes, stirring occasionally, until sausage is cooked through.
2. Add the tomatoes, wine, bay leaves, and sugar.
3. Bring to a boil. Add the clams, cover, and cook until the clams have opened, approximately 4 – 5 minutes.
4. Discard the bay leaves and any unopened clams.
5. Season to taste with salt & pepper.
6. Serve in large bowls with plenty of the broth for bread dipping.
7. Garnish with sprinkles of freshly chopped parsley and lemon wedges, and serve with big chunks of crusty bread and a glass of chardonnay.

*Makes 4 portions*

# Tomato Basil Pasta Sauce

**Full colour photo available at www.chefdez.com**

*"Fresh basil leaves are very fragile and bruise easily, so the best way to cut them is to stack a number of leaves together, roll them up like a cigar, and then slice them into thin ribbons – this is called chiffonade"*

3 tbsp olive oil
1 medium/large carrot, diced very small
2 large celery stalks, diced very small
1 medium white onion, diced very small
6 cloves of garlic, minced
Salt & pepper
1 – 156ml can tomato paste

1 – 796ml can of diced tomatoes
1 cup of full-bodied red wine
½ (one half) cup concentrated vegetable broth, or 1 tsp vegetable paste
2 tbsp white sugar
½ (one half) tsp sambal oelek
Salt & fresh cracked pepper to taste
2 large handfuls fresh basil leaves, chiffonade cut (sliced in thin ribbons)
More fresh basil leaves, for garnish
Grated Parmesan cheese, for garnish

1.  Heat a large heavy bottomed pot over medium to medium-high heat.
2.  Add the olive oil.
3.  Add carrot, celery, onion, and garlic. Gently season with salt & pepper, and cook until soft but not brown, about 3 - 5 minutes; stirring frequently.
4.  Stir in the tomato paste.
5.  Stir in the can of tomatoes (not drained), wine, vegetable broth, sugar, and sambal oelek.
6.  Bring to a boil. Reduce until desired consistency is reached; stirring occasionally; approximately 5 – 10 minutes.
7.  Remove from the heat and season to taste. Toss in the fresh cut basil and serve immediately with your favorite pasta. Garnish with the parmesan cheese and whole basil leaves.

*Makes approximately 6 cups*

# 7

## The "F" Word in the Kitchen is "Flavour"

Hard-nosed Chef Gordon Ramsey has enthralled many with his repeated seasons of TV's reality show "Hell's Kitchen". Although his language is somewhat colourful, to say the least; the "F" word we should focus on in the kitchen is "Flavour".

Countless consumers have frequented restaurants and fallen in love with tastes that they desire to duplicate in their home kitchens. The attempts to do so can often be disappointing. This is most likely due to short cuts that people take when choosing ingredients that fit their lifestyles and time limitations.

For example, I have come across a number of homes that have the large container of peeled, pre-chopped, brine-soaked garlic in their refrigerators. The attractive price and convenience are the catalysts for allowing products like these to enter our homes, but in reality we are sacrificing flavour. Complimenting garlic flavour in a recipe is best achieved by using fresh garlic that has been peeled and prepared at the time the meal is created. Fine restaurants will use the freshest, most high quality ingredients available to enhance the dishes they serve, to bring our palates alive with flavour.

Lemon juice is another common short cut. Lemon juice comes from lemons, not from a bottle. The taste difference in freshness is incredible. Also by utilizing fresh citrus fruits in recipes, one can take advantage of the essential oils in the outer zest of lemons, limes, oranges, and grapefruit.

Bouillon cubes/powders are another ingredient that I find in homes that baffle me. Beef or chicken broth comes from, you guessed it, beef or chicken – not artificial ingredients. Upon examination of these cubes or powders you will notice that the first ingredient isn't even meat derived. There are convenient flavour bases available in better forms at your local supermarket, such as canned condensed broth or, better yet, jarred pastes.

There are many ways of creating flavour in recipes, like marinating meats for example, but the best way is to make a conscious decision to make sure every ingredient in a recipe is the most flavourful choice possible. Speaking of marinating meats – you guessed it – you should not be using powdered meat marinades. A fantastic and quick meat marinade recipe made from "real" ingredients is in my book *Chef Dez on Cooking, Volume One* available for purchase on my website – you will never go back to powder.

> Dear Chef Dez:
>
> I read somewhere that chicken cannot be left in marinade too long. Is there any rule of thumb for this? I know beef and red meats can be in marinade for a long time.
>
> Marj B.
> Abbotsford, BC

> Dear Marj:
>
> This is correct.
>
> Marinades are made up from a base, an acid, and flavourful ingredients. The base of a marinade is usually oil, as this will aid in the cooking process. An acid such as vinegar, wine, or lemon juice is added to breakdown the tougher proteins found in the meat. Red meats and pork, depending on the cuts, are the toughest and are better to marinate from one hour up to twenty-four hours. Chicken proteins are much more delicate and are more preferably marinated for four to six hours. Over marinated chicken will become tough because the acid in the marinade will actually start to cook the more delicate proteins. The same follows through with seafood, as its protein composition is even more fragile than chicken. Seafood should usually be marinated for a mere 30 minutes to one hour when using an acid marinade.

# Fiery Asian Grilled Pork Chops

**Full colour photo available at www.chefdez.com**

*"By cooking the residual marinade into a reduction glaze to finish the chops, they become so delectably delicious and scream with flavor"*

¼ (one quarter) cup Splenda granulated sweetener
¼ (one quarter) cup soy sauce
6 – 8 garlic cloves, crushed
1 tbsp fresh minced ginger
1 tbsp sambal oelek (crushed chili paste/liquid)
1 tsp sesame oil
4 - 6 boneless pork loin center chops, approx. 700g total
1 – 2 green onions, sliced diagonally, for garnish
White and/or black sesame seeds, for garnish

1. Combine Splenda, soy sauce, garlic, ginger, sambal oelek, and sesame oil. Add the pork chops and toss thoroughly. Cover or put in a sealed freezer bag and marinate in the refrigerator for 1 to 6 hours, tossing occasionally.
2. Preheat bar-be-que grill with a high flame. Remove chops from the marinade and put the residual marinade in a small pot.
3. Cook the pork chops on the grill over a medium flame until cooked through, approximately 4 to 7 minutes per side depending on the thickness of the chops and temperature of the grill.
4. Boil the residual marinade at a full boil for approximately 1 to 2 minutes.
5. Brush the cooked marinade onto the pork chops once they have been flipped on the grill.
6. Serve each pork chop garnished with a few green onion slices and a sprinkle of sesame seeds.

*Makes 4 to 6 portions*

# Garlic Gewurztraminer Fudge

**Full colour photo available at www.chefdez.com**

*"Don't be afraid to try this. The garlic adds a slight savoury taste that will keep them guessing. This is the perfect accompaniment on a fruit & cheese platter at a wine & cheese party."*

4 tbsp butter
6 garlic cloves, peeled and cut in half
¼ (one quarter) cup whipping cream
¼ (one quarter) cup Gewurztraminer or other white wine
2 cups white granulated sugar
¼ (one quarter) tsp salt

1. Put all ingredients in a small heavy bottomed pot.
2. Turn heat to low and cook for about 15 – 20 minutes, stirring occasionally, until the sugar is almost completely dissolved.
3. Pick out the garlic clove halves and discard them.
4. At the same temperature, bring the sugar mixture to a rolling boil, stirring frequently until it turns gold in colour – about 20 – 25 minutes. At this point, a drop of the sugar mixture into cold water should solidify and not turn the water cloudy.
5. Remove from the heat and let sit for 5 minutes.
6. Beat vigorously with a wooden spoon until the sugar <u>starts</u> to solidify on the sides of the pot. Then pour into a shallow pan lined with parchment paper and let cool at room temperature.
7. Break or cut into chunks and serve with an assortment of fruit and cheeses, with chilled Gewurztraminer.

# Greek Rack of Lamb

4 racks of lamb approximately 340g each, frenched
2/3 (two thirds) cup olive oil
1/3 (one cup) cup fresh lemon juice
1 tbsp white wine vinegar
3 garlic cloves, crushed
1 tbsp dried oregano (leaves, not ground)
2-3 bay leaves, crumbled
Salt and pepper to season

1. Place lamb in a large freezer bag.
2. Mix all other ingredients in a bowl, and pour into bag of lamb.
3. Seal the bag leaving as little air as possible; toss around to coat.
4. Let marinate in fridge for 1 - 3 hours, tossing around occasionally.
5. Preheat oven to 450 degrees.
6. Preheat heavy bottomed pan over medium/high heat. Remove racks from marinade and remove all bits of bay leaves. When pan is hot, sear the racks on both sides and ends, approximately 5 minutes total.
7. Place the racks in a pan on a wire rack and roast for 15 minutes (approximately for medium rare).
8. Remove the lamb from the oven and let rest for at least 5 minutes before cutting to help allow the meat to retain its juices.

*Makes 8 half-rack servings.*

# "No – Cook" Sweet & Sour Sauce

*"Great for the kids to mix up while you're baking their chicken strips. The ingredient "ketjap manis" is basically sweet soy sauce – look for it at your local Asian grocery or down the Asian foods aisle in your major supermarket. If you can't find it you can substitute it with 3 teaspoons of soy sauce mixed with 2 teaspoons of sugar."*

½ (one half) cup ketchup
3 tablespoons golden corn syrup
2 tablespoons white vinegar
1 tablespoon ketjap manis
2 teaspoons mayonnaise
Pinch of salt

1. Mix together and keep refrigerated.

# Oven Roasted Tomato Soup

*"If you love tomato soup, but not all of the fat that is in traditional tomato cream soup, you will love this recipe! Roasting all of the vegetables really brings out the flavour. If you don't have an immersion hand-blender, then a food processor or blender will work as well."*

1kg ripe Roma tomatoes
1 head of garlic, peeled, cloves separated and left whole
1 small-medium onion, rough chopped
2 tbsp olive oil
2 tbsp balsamic vinegar
1 tbsp dried oregano leaves
1 tbsp dried basil leaves
1 tsp white sugar
Salt and fresh cracked pepper
2 cups of chicken stock

1. Preheat oven to 450 degrees.
2. Cut Roma tomatoes in half lengthwise.

3. In a large bowl toss the tomato halves, garlic and onion with the oil, vinegar, oregano, basil, sugar, and season with salt and pepper.
4. Empty this mixture onto a large baking sheet and arrange the tomatoes cut-side down. If the baking sheet is too crowded you may want to roast them in two batches – over crowding will prevent the vegetable from caramelizing as much as they should.
5. Bake for approximately 35 to 40 minutes until the vegetables are cooked and caramelized.
6. Transfer these ingredients to a large pot, add the chicken stock and puree with an immersion hand-blender. Bring to desired temperature over medium heat while stirring occasionally. Re-season to taste with salt, pepper and sugar.
7. Serve immediately.

*Makes approximately 4 to 5 cups*

# War Udon Noodle Soup

*"Just like the classic War Wonton Soup but made with udon noodles instead"*

1.5 litres chicken stock/broth
1 tsp sesame oil
3 thin slices of fresh ginger
1 carrot, sliced thin diagonally
1kg large prawns, peeled and deveined
1 to 2 cups fresh snow peas
1 small can sliced water chestnuts, drained
1 can baby corn cobs, drained
6 to 12 baby bok choy
2 - 200g packages fresh udon noodles
Salt & pepper, optional
1 bunch green onions, sliced diagonally

1. In a large pot, bring the chicken broth to a boil with the oil and ginger.
2. Reduce the heat to medium and add the carrot slices. Wait 1 minute and then add all of the remaining ingredients, except for the green onions.

3. Continue to cook until the prawns have turned pink and the vegetables are just cooked, approximately 1 to 3 minutes. Taste and season with salt & pepper if needed.
4. Dish out evenly and garnish with green onion slices.

# 8

## *Cooking With or Without Adding Water*

How many recipes have you seen that list water as an ingredient? A pasta sauce recipe, for example, may say to add a cup of water. How much flavour does water have? None. I am always preaching to be innovative while cooking and add ingredients other than water such as wine, broth, beer, juice, etc because they have more flavour. Although most can, some recipes cannot adapt to this type of modification. It will usually depend on the amount of seasonings/flavour already in the dish.

The first thing to examine is the amount of water the recipe suggests. If the amount is of minuscule proportion, then typically replacing the water shouldn't be a concern. The choice of distinctive liquid would accent the existing flavours without risk of overpowering of the dish.

If the recipe states a large quantity of water, then one must examine what the other ingredients are and how much flavour they will impart on their own. This is not as complicated as it may sound. The most effective way to determine if a recipe can accept any variation is to make it the way it is written first and then listen to your taste buds. Could it use more flavour? If so, what would compliment it and how pungent/mellow can the liquid be? Maybe just replacing a portion of the water would be the solution or leaving the recipe in its original state is just fine. Make notes in your cookbooks for future reference.

Rice cooked in chicken stock, for example, has more flavour than if it was cooked in only water. I know that may seem quite obvious, so let me give you some ideas with the following liquids:

**Red Wine or Dark Beer** are great additions to red meat and tomato dishes, such as pasta sauce, gravies, chili, stir-fry's, soups, stews, etc. A general 'rule of thumb' is the stronger the flavours in a certain dish, then the more robust wine/beer it can handle as an ingredient.

**White Wine** is better suited to cream sauces, poultry gravies, lighter soups, and seafood.

**Broth, Stock, or Vegetable Juices** can be paired up with certain dishes, based on the flavours you want to impart, albeit chicken, beef or vegetable. Broth/stock is an option for almost any savoury dish.

**Fruit Juices** can also be used in savoury dishes (savoury is the opposite of sweet). A delicious example would be an orange ginger stir-fry made from orange juice. These are only suggestions as there are countless options and combinations to try. Keep tasting and taking notes. Your cookbooks may turn our looking like high-school textbooks, but for the sake of better eating – it is worth it.

> *Dear Chef Dez:*
> *If I don't have white wine and a recipe calls for it as an ingredient, what can I use instead?*
>
> > *Tim M.*
> > *Nanaimo, BC*
>
> *Dear Tim:*
> *If you want to keep the recipe tasting as close to the way it was written then I would suggest white grape juice or apple juice, as long as the quantity is minimal. The main consideration with fruit juices is their higher sugar content could drastically affect the outcome of the recipe. Therefore it is better to use them in smaller quantities, unless your goal is a sweet finish.*
> *Darker berry & grape juices can also be used in small amounts in place of red wine.*

# Easiest Mussels Recipe Ever

**Full colour photo available at www.chefdez.com**

*"If you love mussels, what could be easier?"*

1 – 430ml jar of store bought salsa
1 – 355ml can of beer
60 – 100 live mussels

1.  Add the salsa and beer to a large pan and bring to a boil over high heat.
2.  Add the live, cleaned, mussels to the pan. Cover and cook until the mussels have steamed open, approximately 2 minutes.
3.  Discard any mussels that didn't open and then serve the mussels with the broth and big chunks of crusty bread... and a mug of beer (optional, of course).


# Drunken Pig

**Full colour photo available at www.chefdez.com**

*"Lots of pork with lots of wine! Perfect when served with my recipe for Garlic Mashed Potatoes – see this chapter."*

Salt & pepper
1.5 kg pork butt roast
2 tbsp olive oil
1 medium onion, diced small
6 – 8 garlic cloves, minced
1 ½ (one and one half) cups and a splash of red wine
2 sprigs fresh rosemary (plus more for garnish)
1 bay leaf
2 tbsp tomato paste
2 tsp white sugar
Salt & fresh cracked pepper to taste, if desired
1-2 tsp butter (optional)

1. Remove the string from roast, and cut into 3 or 4 equal pieces.
2. Lightly season roast pieces with salt and pepper.
3. Heat a heavy bottomed pan over medium-high heat.
4. Add oil to pan and brown the pork on all sides, in two batches if using a smaller pan.
5. Remove the pork and set aside.
6. Cool down the pan a bit, and sauté the onion and garlic over medium heat for about 2 minutes until softened a bit.
7. Deglaze the pan with a splash of wine.
8. Add the pork, rosemary, bay leaf, and 1-½ cups of wine to the pan; bring to a boil over high heat.
9. Turn down to simmer; cover and cook over med-low heat for 2 hours. *Half way through the cooking time, flip the pork pieces over.
10. Remove the pork and set aside covered with foil to keep warm. Discard the Bay leaf and the rosemary sprigs.
11. Increase the heat to high, add the tomato paste and the sugar, and reduce the liquid for about 10-15 minutes until syrupy.
12. Taste and adjust seasonings if needed.
13. Finish the sauce by removing from heat and stirring in butter until just melted (optional).
14. Cut the pork into bite-sized pieces or slices.
15. Serve immediately; plate a mound of "Garlic Mashed Potatoes" in the center with a few pork pieces on top. Drizzle a couple tablespoons of sauce over the pork and on the plate around the mashed potatoes.
16. Garnish with freshly chopped parsley and a sprig of fresh rosemary.

*Serves 6 to 8 people with "Garlic Mashed Potatoes"*

## Garlic Mashed Potatoes

*"These will spoil you for any other mashed potatoes – very rich and flavourful"*

5 russet potatoes, peeled and diced approximated one half inch
½ (one half) cup butter, cubed
6 – 8 garlic cloves, crushed

2 tsp salt
½ (one half) tsp pepper
½ (one half) cup whipping cream

1.  Steam potatoes over boiling water for approximately 20 minutes until tender.
2.  Drain water out of the pot, and put cooked potatoes in the pot.
3.  Add the butter, garlic, salt, and pepper.
4.  Mash by hand until almost smooth.
5.  Add the cream and mash again until smooth.
6.  Taste and re-season with salt & pepper if necessary.

*Makes approximately 6 – 8 portions*

# Soft Polenta

*"A classic staple of Italy. This recipe is so good I have even had old Italian women tell me it's the best polenta they have ever eaten! Serve on its own as a side dish, or as you would pasta with a tomato sauce."*

4 cups water
1 Tbsp salt
4 cups milk
½ (one half) cup butter
2 cups yellow cornmeal
100g Romano cheese, grated
2-3 garlic cloves, crushed

1.  Bring water and salt to a boil in a heavy bottomed pot.
2.  Add the milk and butter and heat over medium heat until butter is melted and mixture is almost at a boil again, stirring occasionally.
3.  Add the cornmeal gradually while stirring constantly.
4.  Continue stirring until mixture starts to become thick. Reduce heat to medium-low and stir constantly for 3 to 5 minutes, until it has reached desired consistency. It should be the same thickness as porridge.

5. Remove from the heat and stir in the Romano cheese and garlic thoroughly.
6. Serve immediately, alone or with your favorite pasta sauce.

*Makes approximately 9 cups*

# Hop'n Shrimp Gumbo

**Full colour photo available at www.chefdez.com**

*"Classic gumbo made with beer and shrimp. The okra adds body to this wonderful New Orleans style soup."*

3 tbsp olive oil
2 large celery stalks, diced small
1 large red bell pepper, diced small
1 medium-large onion, diced small
6 garlic cloves, minced
2 tsp paprika
2 tsp sugar
1 ½ (one and one half) tsp dried thyme leaves
1 tsp salt
½ (one half) tsp pepper
½ (one half) tsp ground cayenne pepper
1 – 250g bag frozen okra, thawed, & sliced into ¼ inch rings
2 – 355ml cans of beer
1 – 284ml can condensed chicken broth
½ (one half) cup dry orzo pasta
Juice of 1 lemon
454g (1 pound) cooked small shrimp
Fresh thyme sprigs, for garnish
Zest of 1 lemon

1. Heat a heavy bottomed pot over medium heat.
2. Add the oil and them the celery, bell pepper, onion, garlic, paprika, sugar, dried thyme, salt, pepper, and cayenne pepper. Cook for 2 – 3 minutes until soft, stirring occasionally.

3.  Add the okra and continue to cook for 2 – 3 minutes until the okra starts to get sticky.

4.  Slowly stir in the beer. Stir in the condensed chicken broth. Turn the heat to high and bring to a boil.

5.  Stir in the orzo pasta and simmer uncovered over medium-low heat for approximately 6 – 8 minutes until the pasta is cooked.

6.  Remove from the heat and stir in the lemon juice and the shrimp and serve immediately, with each bowl garnished with a fresh thyme sprig and lemon zest.

*Makes 4 – 6 servings*

# 9
## Cooking Pasta for the Best Results

A staple in almost every home's pantry is spaghetti or some form of pasta that makes its way to the dinner table on a regular basis. Many of us take the time to focus on building the flavour and complexity of the accompanying sauce for our pasta of choice; however the pasta itself needs attention as well. Many food columns could be dedicated to achieving palate-pleasing goals in pasta sauces, but let us not forget about the substance of these dishes – the pasta noodle. Thus this column will be focused on unraveling some myths and procedures in what seems to be one of the simplest tasks in the kitchen – boiling water and cooking pasta.

The first thing to examine is the dry pasta noodle and the transformation that takes place during the cooking process. The most obvious observation is that cooked pasta is larger in volume and flexible, compared to dry raw pasta. What makes this possible is the absorption of water during the boiling process. The cooking process of any food, no matter how simple it seems, needs to be analyzed because this is our chance of infusing flavour into the ingredients being cooked.

Everyone has heard of the process of salting water when boiling pasta, but few know or realize the reason why. Some believe it is to help the pasta from sticking or to help keep the water from boiling over; however the reason is to season the pasta and to increase the flavour. Pasta on its own is very bland, and combining bland cooked pasta with a sauce that you have perfected, will be a detriment to your finished dish. If the pasta water is salted liberally then the pasta will be absorbing salt-water, instead of just water, and thus your pasta dish will be seasoned from the inside out.

Another no-no is to add oil to your pasta water. This idea probably first came about to prevent the pasta noodles from sticking together, however it will affect your finished dish negatively. Oiled pasta water will help to keep your pasta from sticking together when cooking, but a film of oil will always be left on the drained noodles. This thin film of oil will inhibit the starchiness of the cooked pasta and then in turn lead to the accompanying sauce to not stick to or absorb into the noodles as much. When pasta is eaten you want the starchiness of the pasta to hold onto the sauce as much as possible, so that the dish will be able to be enjoyed to the fullest. That being said, drained cooked pasta should not be oiled for the same reason.

A better way to help prevent your pasta noodles from sticking together during the cooking process is to stir the noodles constantly for the first two minutes of cooking time. By that point the water will have returned to its full-boil action and the agitation of the bubbling water will keep the pasta moving and prevent it from sticking.

Once the pasta has been drained, do not rinse it. Rinsing will cool the pasta down and also wash away some of the starchiness that we want to help secure the sauce to the noodles.

Homemade "spaghetti" is a very common dish in many households, and whether you use spaghetti, linguine, or other types of noodles, I hope these few simple recommendations help to make your meal more enjoyable and flavourful.

> Dear Chef Dez:
> What is the best way to tell when pasta is cooked?
>
> > Norma L.
> > Maple Ridge, BC

> Dear Norma:
> There are many ways that people use to determine that pasta is cooked to perfection – including the old wives' tale about throwing it against the wall, and if it sticks, it's done. The best way is to let your mouth do the talking. Carefully remove a strand or piece of pasta from the boiling water. After waiting a few seconds to cool down, take a bite. It should feel 'el dente,' meaning 'to the tooth' in Italian. This relates to the feeling that the pasta should not be overcooked and offer some resistance when biting into it. It should not be hard, but should not be too soft and mushy either.
> The package of the pasta you purchase will always offer a guideline cooking time, but your bite will always give you the right answer.

# Basil Ricotta Pasta Filling

**Full colour photo available at www.chefdez.com**

*"Perfect for all stuffed pastas – ravioli, tortellini, etc"*

2 cups ricotta cheese
1 cup finely grated Parmesan cheese
¼ (one quarter) cup basil leaves, chopped fine
2 cloves of garlic, crushed to a paste
½ (one half) tsp salt
Pepper (a few grinds of a pepper mill)

1. Mix all ingredients together and use to fill pasta.

Notes: Tortellini is best made from either a 2.5 or 3 inch round cutter with one half teaspoon of filling and cook for approximately 5 minutes. Ravioli use approximately a rounded teaspoon of filling for each, and cook for approximately 3 minutes.

# Fresh Pasta from Scratch

**Full colour photo available at www.chefdez.com**

*"What a wonderfully rustic thing to create from raw ingredients! It cooks fast and tastes incredible with your favourite pasta sauce."*

2 ¾ (two and three quarters) cups all-purpose flour
3 large eggs
¼ (one quarter) cup + 1 tbsp + 1 tsp water
1 tbsp extra virgin olive oil
Salt

1. Mound the flour on a countertop and make a well in the center large enough for the rest of the ingredients.
2. Add the eggs, water, oil and a pinch of salt to the well. Scramble the eggs with a fork and slowly start incorporating the flour. Keep mixing with

a fork while continuing to incorporate more flour until you cannot mix with a fork any longer. Continue to mix by hand for a couple of minutes until it comes together in one mass. You may need to add a bit more water if it is too dry or a bit more flour if it is too wet. It should be firm and holding together but not sticky.

3.  Knead by hand for approximately 8 to 10 minutes until smooth. Shape into a ball, cover with plastic wrap and let sit at room temperature for 30 to 45 minutes. Or alternatively up to 3 hours in the refrigerator.

4.  Cut dough into 4 equal pieces and work with one piece at a time while keeping the others covered. Set your pasta machine to the widest setting. Hand shape the piece of dough into an approximate rectangle and feed it through the machine. Fold it over and pass it through again, and do this a couple of times to help make it as rectangular as possible.

5.  Continue to run it through the machine while narrowing the rollers on the pasta machine each time. You may have to fold it in half a couple of times to help keep the rectangular shape as you go along.

6.  Stop when the pasta has reached the desired thickness, dust liberally with flour and cut into the desired shape(s). Dust one more time with flour and set aside covered with plastic wrap until all the pasta dough is rolled and cut.

7.  Bring salted water to a boil and then add the fresh pasta, stirring immediately and cook until done – anywhere from 2 to 6 minutes depending on the thickness you have chosen. Toss with your favorite sauce and enjoy!

*Makes approximately one and a half pounds of fresh pasta*

## *Minestrone*

**Full colour photo available at www.chefdez.com**

*"Classic Italian vegetable soup at its finest! Make sure to cut all the vegetables in small uniform sizes for attractiveness and variety in each spoonful. Pancetta (Italian bacon) would be more classic, but I prefer the smokiness of regular bacon in this recipe."*

250g bacon slices, sliced into ¼ (one quarter) inch pieces
1 medium onion, diced ¼ (one quarter) inch

1 medium carrot, diced ¼ (one quarter) inch

2 celery stalks, diced ¼ (one quarter) inch

6 garlic cloves, minced

½ (one half) tsp salt

¼ (one quarter) tsp pepper

2 stalks fresh rosemary, chopped

1 chunk of parmesan rind

1 cup white wine

1 – 796ml can diced tomatoes

4 cups vegetable broth

3 bay leaves

1 ½ (one and one half) cups ¼ (one quarter) inch diced butternut squash

1 small zucchini, diced ¼ (one quarter) inch, approximately 2 cups

¾ (three quarters) cup dry orzo pasta

1 – 540ml can Romano beans or kidney beans, drained & rinsed

1 ½ (one and one half) tsp sugar

¼ (one quarter) cup chopped fresh parsley

Salt & pepper to season

Parmigiano Reggiano cheese, shaved for garnish

1. In a large pot over medium/high heat, cook the bacon pieces until crisp, stirring occasionally. Remove with a slotted spoon and set aside while leaving the rendered bacon fat in the pan.

2. Turn the heat to medium and add the onion, carrot, celery, garlic, salt, pepper, rosemary and cook for approximately 2 to 3 minutes until softened a bit, stirring occasionally.

3. Add the parmesan rind, wine, tomatoes, 4 cups of the broth, bay leaves, squash, and zucchini.

4. Turn the heat to high and bring to a boil. Add the orzo, reduce the heat to medium/high and continue to cook uncovered until the orzo has cooked to al dente, approximately 6 to 8 minutes, stirring occasionally.

5. Remove from the heat and add the beans, sugar and parsley. Season to taste with salt and pepper, and remove & discard the parmesan rind and bay leaves.

6. Garnish each bowl with shavings of Parmigiano Reggiano and the reserved bacon pieces.

*Makes approximately 3 litres*

# White Sauce

*"For extra depth of flavour, onion and cloves are infused with the milk."*

5 tbsp butter
6 tbsp flour
2.5 - 3 cups milk
1 medium onion, peeled and halved
10 whole cloves
½ - 1 tsp salt
¼ (one quarter) tsp ground white pepper
Pinch of ground nutmeg

1. In a heavy bottomed saucepan melt the butter over low heat and add flour. Cook for approximately 2 to 3 minutes to remove starchy flavour, stirring occasionally.
2. Pour milk into a microwave safe container.
3. Stud the cut onion with the whole cloves. Submerse onion in milk and microwave until hot.
4. Remove the onion and cloves from the milk.
5. With heat on low, add the milk very slowly into the butter/flower mixture while whisking constantly. It will get extremely thick but it will slowly thin out as the milk is gradually added. Adding the milk too fast will cause lumps in the final sauce.
6. When all of the milk has been incorporated, bring mixture to a boil while whisking constantly (sauce will not be fully thickened until it has reached the boiling point). Remove from heat and season with the salt, pepper, and nutmeg.

*Makes approximately 3 cups*

# 10

## *Quick Breads are Named for Their Convenience*

Some of the simplest baking products to make are quick breads. Quick breads, as the name implies, can be made in a shorter amount of time than traditional yeast breads. Examples would be banana bread, muffins, scones, etc., and although easier, there is still information worth knowing.

The biggest, and most obvious, difference between yeast breads and quick breads is that quick breads are not leavened with yeast. The term "leavening" can be described as the creating and capturing of gases in a baked product to produce structure and height. As yeast ferments, with the help of sugar, it creates gas that causes the holes visible in bread. Quick breads rely on leaveners such as baking soda, baking powder, steam, eggs and air to give a similar effect.

Baking soda and baking powder are considered chemical leaveners. Baking soda is *sodium bicarbonate* and it requires liquid and an acid to make a gaseous reaction. It is usually added to recipes that have a naturally occurring acid in the ingredients. This acid can be found in items such as buttermilk, yogurt, sour cream, honey, molasses, and fruits. The amount of baking soda used is determined and balanced by the amount of these acids occurring in the recipe's ingredients.

Baking powder on the other hand is a complete leavener, as it only requires liquid for it to react in the same manner. The reason for this is that it contains a mixture of baking soda and the balanced amount of acid, along with starch to help prevent lumping. This is why you will see some recipes that call for baking powder and others with baking powder and/or baking soda. A good comparison of this would be a pancake recipe compared to a buttermilk pancake recipe.

Most quick bread recipes consist of mixing dry and wet ingredients in two separate bowls first before combining them.

Not only are quick breads fast, they are also very tender. This is due to the limited production of gluten in the mixing process. When flour and liquid are mixed together, gluten is formed. Gluten is most recognizable as the elastic feeling in yeast bread dough that has been kneaded. The longer that flour and liquid are mixed, the more gluten is created. Quick breads are similar to the texture of cakes and thus one should not over-mix to ensure a delicate composition.

Regardless of which chemical leaveners you use, the batter should go into the oven immediately once mixed together, as the gases start producing immediately when the liquid is added. If using eggs and air to leaven, bake immediately before it deflates, for optimal results.

Once in the oven, heat will convert moisture in the batter to steam. The steam, air and gasses from leavening will be trapped in the batter, thus giving the product height and a fluffy texture.

> Dear Chef Dez:
>
> I love pancakes, but whenever I make them they turn out tough. I know it's not the recipe because it is the same one that my mom uses and hers always turn out fluffy and delicate. Can you help me?
>
> Sarah D.
> Burnaby, BC
>
> Dear Sarah:
>
> Pancakes are much like quick breads as they should have a cake-like texture, hence the name pan-"cakes". The biggest mistake made when preparing pancake batter is that one tends to over-mix. Over-mixing flour and liquid produces gluten, which will give it more structure. The more mixing one does, the more gluten is created, and the tougher the cooked pancakes will be. It is okay for your batter to be a bit lumpy.
>
> Also, make sure you are not using "bread" flour, as it contains more gluten than all-purpose or pastry flour. I hope this helps.

# Banana Nut Muffins

**Recipe created by Katherine Desormeaux (Mrs. Chef Dez)**

2 cups whole wheat flour

1 cup brown sugar

1 tsp baking soda

1 tsp cinnamon

½ (one half) tsp nutmeg

½ (one half) tsp cloves

½ (one half) tsp salt

½ (one half) cup chopped nuts

2 eggs, beaten

2 ½ (two and one half) cups mashed bananas

½ (one half) cup canola oil

1 tsp grated lemon zest

1 tsp vanilla extract

1. Preheat oven to 350 degrees and prepare an 18-cup muffin tin with baking spray.
2. Combine the flour, sugar, baking soda, cinnamon, nutmeg, cloves, and salt together in a bowl. Toss in the chopped nuts of your choice.
3. In a separate bowl combine the eggs, bananas, oil, lemon zest, and vanilla together.
4. Add the wet ingredients to the dry ingredients and mix until just combined. DO NOT OVERMIX.
5. Divide batter equally into the 18 muffins cups and bake for approximately 20 -25 minutes. Cool 5 minutes in the pan before removing to a wire rack to cool completely.

*Makes 18 muffins*

# Blueberry Bran Muffins

**Full colour photo available at www.chefdez.com**

Recipe created by Katherine Desormeaux (Mrs. Chef Dez)

*"Tossing the blueberries in the mixture of dry ingredients will help keep them suspended in the batter instead of sinking to the bottom"*

1 cup whole wheat flour

1 cup natural bran

1 tsp baking powder

1 tsp baking soda

½ (one half) tsp salt

1 cup blueberries

1 egg, beaten

1/3 (one third) cup canola oil

¼ (one quarter) cup brown sugar

3 tbsp maple syrup

1 tsp vanilla extract

1 cup buttermilk or sour milk *see note below

1. Preheat oven to 375 degrees and prepare a 12-cup muffin tin with baking spray.
2. Combine the flour, bran, baking powder, baking soda, and salt together in a bowl. Toss in the blueberries.
3. In a separate bowl combine the egg, oil, sugar, syrup, vanilla, and buttermilk together.
4. Add the wet ingredients to the dry ingredients and mix until just combined. DO NOT OVERMIX.
5. Divide batter equally into the 12 muffins cups and bake for approximately 20 -25 minutes. Cool 5 minutes in the pan before removing to a wire rack to cool completely.

*Makes 12 muffins*

*Note: Sour milk can be easily made by putting one teaspoon of lemon juice or vinegar into a one cup measure. Fill cup with milk and let sit for two minutes.

# Ham and Cheddar Scones

Recipe created by Katherine Desormeaux (Mrs. Chef Dez)

*"This is Dez's favourite breakfast. Omit the ham to make cheese scones or omit both ham and cheese for plain scones. You can add raisins or fresh blueberries to the plain scone."*

2 cups all purpose flour
½ (one half) cup granulated sugar
½ (one half) tsp salt
1 tbsp baking powder
½ (one half) tsp baking soda
½ (one half) cup very cold or frozen butter
¾ (three quarters) cup old cheddar cut into quarter inch cubes
¾ (three quarters) cup ham cut into ¼ inch cubes
¾ (three quarters) cup butter milk
2 tbsp whipping cream, optional

1. Preheat the oven to 375 degrees.
2. Prepare a jelly roll pan or two cookie sheets with baking spray.
3. Combine flour, sugar, salt, baking powder and baking soda in a large bowl. Using a medium fine grater, grate the butter into the flour mixture, stirring occasionally to coat the butter pieces in flour. Toss in the ham and cheddar cubes to coat with flour.
4. Add the butter milk and stir only enough to moisten. DO NOT OVER MIX.
5. Divide dough in half. Directly on the baking sheet, form each half of the dough into a 6 inch flat circle approximately 1 inch thick. Sprinkle the dough lightly with flour as necessary. Take the time to make neat smooth sides and surfaces.
6. Cut each disk into 6 wedges, but don't separate the wedges from each other – the support from the scones being side-by-side will help them rise better. Optional – brush the tops with the whipping cream for a shinier finish.
7. Bake for 15 to 20 minutes until golden brown.
8. Immediately upon removing from the oven recut the scones on the score lines. Cool for 5 minutes on the pan.

*Makes 12 scones*

# Health Nut Pancakes

Recipe written by Katherine Desormeaux (Mrs. Chef Dez)

*"Buttermilk has a thicker consistency, so if you choose to use skim milk instead you don't need as much"*

1 cup whole wheat flour
¼ (one quarter) cup wheat germ
¼ (one quarter) cup ground almonds
2 tbsp sesame seeds
2 tbsp ground flax seed
2 tbsp sugar
1 tbsp baking powder
½ (one half) tsp salt
1 egg, beaten
2 cups buttermilk, or 1 ½ (one and one half) cups skim milk
1 tbsp canola oil

1. Combine the flour, wheat germ, almonds, sesame seeds, flax, sugar, baking powder, and salt in a large mixing bowl.
2. In a separate smaller bowl, combine the egg, buttermilk, and canola oil together.
3. Preheat a non-stick pan or griddle over medium heat.
4. Pour the wet ingredients into the dry ingredients and mix until just combined – DO NOT OVERMIX.
5. With a large ladle, pour a portion of the batter onto the hot pan. Once bubbles form and start to pop on the surface of the pancakes, flip over to cook the other side until golden brown.

*Makes approximately 8 to 10 four-inch pancakes.*

# Popovers

Recipe created by Katherine Desormeaux (Mrs. Chef Dez)

*"These are a favourite with our family – either as a side with dinner, or for breakfast with butter and honey. For the flour use either all-purpose flour, or 50% all-purpose and 50% whole wheat – using all whole wheat flour will make them too heavy."*

4 eggs, beaten
1 ½ (one and one half) cups milk
1 ½ (one and one half) cups flour
1 tsp salt
2 tbsp butter

1.  Preheat oven to 375 degrees and grease the cups of a 12-cup muffin tin heavily with the 2 tbsp butter.
2.  Whisk the eggs and milk together. Add the flour & salt and continue whisking until combined (some lumps are fine).
3.  Divide the mixture evenly into the muffin cups and bake for 25 to 30 minutes until golden brown. DO NOT OPEN THE OVEN DURING THE BAKING PROCESS OR THE POPOVERS WILL DEFLATE.
4.  After removing them from the oven, pierce each popover with a fork to allow the steam to escape.

*Variation: Try adding crushed garlic to the batter and sprinkling tops with parmesan cheese, or rosemary to the batter and cheddar cheese on top.

*Makes 12 popovers*

# Spiced Apple Loaf

**Full colour photo available at www.chefdez.com**

Recipe created by Katherine Desormeaux (Mrs. Chef Dez)

*"Use 1 cup whole wheat flour and 1 cup all-purpose, or 2 cups all-purpose – but using 2 cups whole wheat flour will make the loaf too heavy"*

1 cup whole wheat flour

1 cup all-purpose flour

1 ½ (one and one half) tsp cinnamon

1 tsp baking powder

½ (one half) tsp baking soda

½ (one half) tsp salt

¼ (one quarter) tsp nutmeg

¼ (one quarter) tsp cloves

2 apples, peeled & diced ½ to ¾ inch

½ (one half) cup butter, room temperature

1 cup sugar

2 eggs, beaten

2 tsp vanilla

1 cup buttermilk

1. Preheat the oven to 350 degrees and prepare a standard loaf pan with baking spray.
2. Combine the flour, cinnamon, baking powder, baking soda, salt, nutmeg, and cloves together in a bowl. Toss the diced apple into this dry mixture – this will help to keep the apple chunks suspended in the finished batter instead of sinking to the bottom.
3. Beat the butter and sugar together in a separate bowl. Add the eggs, vanilla and butter milk and mix thoroughly together.
4. Add the wet ingredients to the dry ingredients and mix until just combined. DO NOT OVERMIX. Place in the prepared loaf pan and bake for approximately 50 to 60 minutes, or until an inserted wooden skewer comes out clean.
5. Cool 5 minutes in the pan before removing to a wire rack to cool completely.

*Makes 1 loaf*

# Whole Wheat Graham Crackers

**Full colour photo available at www.chefdez.com**

Recipe created by Katherine Desormeaux (Mrs. Chef Dez)

"Graham Flour is actually all purpose flour with a certain amount of wheat bran and wheat germ added back. It is a simple matter to make your own."

1 2/3 (one and two thirds) cups whole wheat flour

1/3 (one third) cup wheat bran

¼ (one quarter) cup wheat germ

½ (one half) cup dark brown sugar, packed

1 tsp baking powder

1 tsp salt

½ (one half) cup cold butter

¼ (one quarter) cup vegetable oil

¼ (one quarter) cup water

1. Preheat the oven to 425 degrees
2. Combine the flour, bran, wheat germ, brown sugar, baking powder and salt in a bowl.
3. Grate or cut in the butter as if for pastry.
4. Mix in the oil and the water.
5. Divide dough in half. Roll the dough directly on the baking sheet as it is too crumbly to transfer after it has been rolled. If your baking sheet has edges turn it over and use the bottom of the cookie sheet. Dust the surface of the pan with flour and continue to dust the top surface with flour as needed. Roll to 1/8 (one eighth) of an inch thickness. Trim edges (reserve to re-roll) and cut into rectangles. It is not necessary to leave spaces between the crackers. Dock each cracker with a fork. Bake for about 10 minutes. If the crackers on the edges are getting too brown, remove them to a wire rack to cool and continue baking the rest. The crackers will not be crisp when warm, but will become crisp as they cool.

*Makes approximately 4 dozen, 2 inch square, crackers.*

# 11

## Easily Incorporate More Fruits & Vegetables in Your Diet

The food guide published by the Canadian Government recommends that we, as adults, should be eating an average of seven to ten servings of fruits and vegetables every day. Children should be eating four to eight servings, depending on their age. January is a popular month for people to start better eating habits, so to assist you I have gathered some helpful ways to fulfill your intake requirements for healthy eating.

The Canada Food Guide describes a single serving of fruit or vegetables as one half cup of fresh, frozen or canned or one half cup of 100% juice. Alternatively one cup of raw leafy vegetables or salads counts as a single serving, as well as a single piece of fruit.

The first and most important direction to lead you in is to ensure that you are buying fruits and vegetables in the first place. Chances are if you don't have them available at your fingertips, you will miss many opportunities to introduce them into your diet: out of sight, out of mind. One helpful tip is to buy the recommended serving amounts for each member of your family for number of days you are shopping for. For example, if you are a family of four and shopping to get you through the next 3 days, you would need to buy a total of 84 servings of fruit and vegetables combined, based on an average of 7 servings each. Purchase these before proceeding to the other departments and isles and build your meals based on these initial produce selections.

An easy way to incorporate fresh spinach with every meal is to serve every piece of chicken or fish on a bed of sautéed spinach leaves. Simply heat a pan over medium heat with a very small amount of olive oil, add a large handful of clean, fresh spinach leaves and season with salt & pepper. They will cook and wilt very quickly as you toss with tongs. Plate and serve immediately.

If sandwiches are a meal item that you have regularly, then make sure you always have fresh lettuce, tomato and onions on hand at all times. A Mediterranean flair can also be added to your sandwiches by including roasted bell peppers or a spread of roasted garlic.

Fruit can become an easily accessible snack item by always having containers of washed berries and grapes in your refrigerator at all times. Try not to pre-wash too much ahead of time however, as they tend to deteriorate faster after washing.

Vegetable skewers on the grill are another low fat way to get your daily servings. Although barbequing during the cold weather is not as popular as the spring and summer months, it does continue to offer low fat cooking if you can rearrange your grill to make it easily accessible.

Even if there is a member of your family that is somewhat fussy when it comes to eating fruits and vegetables, the produce departments seem to always be expanding in selection of imported/exotic goods. Buy something completely new to your family at least once per month. The Internet and libraries are filled with an abundance of information on preparing and serving almost any ingredient. Happy cooking!

*Dear Chef Dez:*
*I am on a diet and looking for ways to add flavour to my meals without adding fat or too many calories. Any suggestions?*

*Dawn W.*
*Langley, BC*

*Dear Dawn:*
*Herbs and spices are the way to go. Dry spice rubs and fresh herbs add a ton of flavour without adding a number of calories. Try cooking with fat-free broths. Wine and juices are great to cook with for flavour, but remember they loaded with natural sugars.*
*Stay away from condiments like ketchup and barbeque sauce, as they are also loaded with sugar.*

# Pineapple Salsa

**Full colour photo available at www.chefdez.com**

Diced fresh Pineapple, approximately 1 ½ (one and one half) cups
1 medium red bell pepper diced small
½ (one half) jalapeno, minced – seeds & membrane removed for a milder salsa
¼ (one quarter) cup small diced red onion
2 – 4 tbsp finely chopped fresh mint
Zest from 1 lime, finely chopped
2 tbsp lime juice
1 ½ (one and one half) tsp sugar
1 tsp fresh cracked black pepper
¼ (one quarter) tsp salt

1.   Mix all ingredients together.

*Makes approximately 2 cups*


# Prawn & Veggie Kabobs

**Full colour photo available at www.chefdez.com**

¼ (one quarter) cup olive oil
¼ (one quarter) cup balsamic vinegar
2 tsp dried oregano leaves
1 tsp dried basil leaves
1 tsp sugar
½ (one half) tsp salt
¼ (one half) tsp fresh cracked pepper
An assortment of veggies, cut into cubes or small pieces*
2 pounds of large raw prawns

1.  Whisk all the ingredients (except for the vegetables and prawns) together in a small bowl.
2.  Place the marinade with the cut vegetables in a large sealable bag and let marinate in the refrigerator for a couple of hours.
3.  For the last 15 minutes of marinating time, add the raw prawns to the bag as well.
4.  Remove all of the veggies and prawns from the bag and skewer onto wood or metal skewers. If using wood skewers make sure that they have been soaked in water for hours to help prevent them from burning on the barbeque.
5.  Cook over a medium-high flame until the prawns are cooked and serve immediately.

'* the veggies can consist of almost anything, but here are some suggestions:
Mushrooms, bell peppers, eggplant, red onion, cherry tomatoes, etc.

# Raspberry Coullis

*"A quick dessert sauce to serve with anything chocolate"*

340g package frozen raspberries, thawed ~ or 1 pint fresh
3 tbsp sugar
2 tsp fresh lemon juice

1.  Puree the raspberries, 3 tbsp sugar, and lemon juice in a food processor. Strain through a fine wire-mesh strainer, pressing firmly with a spatula to get as much pulp as possible while leaving the seeds in the strainer. Discard the seeds. Taste and re-season with more sugar and/or lemon juice if desired.

# Roasted Pepper Eggs Benedict

**Full colour photo available at www.chefdez.com**

*"Using roasted red pepper instead of traditional ham or bacon, makes this inviting to vegetarians.*
*A white cheddar cheese sauce also replaces the classic hollandaise sauce."*

2 large red bell peppers
2 tbsp olive oil
½ (one half) tsp Worcestershire sauce
Pinch of salt
¼ (one quarter) cup butter
¼ (one quarter) cup flour
1 ½ (one and one half) to 2 cups milk
2 cups grated white cheddar
½ (one half) tsp salt
Pinch of ground white pepper
4 large eggs, poached
2 English muffins, split and toasted

1.  Preheat your Bar-be-que with a medium/high flame.
2.  Visualizing the peppers as cubes, cut the 4 sides off each of the bell peppers, and then the bottoms and tops (discarding the stems, inner seeds and membranes). Toss with the olive oil. Place them on the preheated grill and cook until the skins have become somewhat charred, turning the pieces over halfway.
3.  Remove the red peppers from the grill and place in an air-tight covered glass bowl for at least 10 to 20 minutes – the steam from the heat of the peppers will help loosen the skins. Remove the peppers from the bowl - peel and discard the skins.
4.  Reserve 4 of the largest pieces of roasted pepper for the final presentation, while placing the remaining pieces in a food processor. To the food processor also add the Worcestershire sauce and the pinch of salt. Puree on high speed for 30 to 60 seconds. Remove this mixture and press through a fine wire mesh strainer to remove to create a smooth puree. Set this aside as a garnishing sauce.
5.  In a heavy bottomed small saucepan, melt the butter over low heat. Stir in the flour and continue to cook over low heat, stirring occasionally,

to cook the starchy taste out of the flour, approximately 5 to 7 minutes. Add the 1 ½ (one and one half) cups milk very slowly while whisking into the butter/flour mixture. It will get extremely thick at first, but keep working in small amounts of the milk at a time to prevent lumps. Turn the heat to medium once all of the milk has been incorporated. Add the grated cheese and continue to whisk constantly until the mixture thickens and just comes to a boil. If the sauce is too thick then add the extra milk to thin it out. Remove from the heat and set aside. Season with the ½ (one half) teaspoon of salt and the white pepper.

6. Poach the eggs, toast the muffins, and assemble as follows: per serving place one muffin half, one roasted red pepper slice, one egg, top with hot cheese sauce, and garnish with the roasted red pepper sauce.

*Makes four single egg portions*

# Spinach Artichoke Dip

*"Served with tortilla chips, this will be one of the best appetizers at any party"*

1 – 250g package cream cheese, room temperature
1 ½ (one and one half) cups sour cream
1 cup mayonnaise
100g – 150g mozzarella cheese, grated
2 cans artichoke hearts, drained and chopped
2 – 300g packages frozen chopped spinach, thawed and drained
2 garlic cloves, crushed
2 - 3 tbsp red wine vinegar
½ (one half) tsp sambal oelek
Salt & fresh cracked pepper to taste

1. Preheat oven to 350 degrees.
2. Thoroughly combine the sour cream into the cream cheese.
3. Stir in the mayonnaise, mozzarella, artichokes, spinach, garlic, red wine vinegar, and sambal oelek.
4. Season to taste with salt and pepper.

5. Transfer to an oven-proof dish and bake for approximately 50 to 60 minutes until completely heated through. Serve immediately with tortilla chips for dipping.

*Makes approximately 6 cups*

# 12

## *Nutrition and Flavour from Blueberries*

Summertime always offers a bountiful harvest of fresh fruit and berries; and blueberries, are by far, one of my favorite. They are not only packed full of nutrition and flavour but are also a very versatile cooking ingredient.

Upon any investigation into foods that are rich in antioxidants, you will always find berries at the top of the list. Blueberries seem to have all the other berries beat when it comes to antioxidant levels. The health benefits that we gain from foods abundant in antioxidants are too numerous to list in complete detail but includes anti-aging, lower cholesterol, strong immune resistance to flues and viruses, and reduction in risks of cancer and heart disease. This being said, it is in our best interest to attempt to introduce blueberries into our meals whenever possible.

The first idea that crosses most people's minds when considering blueberries as an ingredient is desserts, but blueberries also compliment many savoury dishes quite well. Here are two suggestions for you to experiment with in the kitchen:

**Red Meat** – Since blueberries are very dark and intensely flavoured, they tend to stand up to meats that are also very bold. A red wine pan gravy on steaks, roasted beef, or lamb for example, is always complimented by the rich intensity of a couple handfuls of blueberries cooked down in it. Simply strain out the skins for a smooth syrupy sauce. Many people who have cooked with me also know that I am a big fan of including a dark berry jam into ground meat dishes (chili, meatloaf, hamburgers, etc.) based on this same principle.

**Salads** – When dealing with acids in vinaigrettes, blueberries work well as added sweetness, either as a salad ingredient or pureed into the dressing, to help tone down the sharp notes of vinegars, lemon, and lime juices. The result is a smoother more complex taste.

One last thing to remember is that blueberries are also enhanced by the taste of balsamic vinegar. Try this at home tonight: take a handful of blueberries, wash and dry them, and toss with a teaspoon of balsamic, and a sprinkle of sugar, if desired. The blueberries and the balsamic are both bold flavours and match up quite well. Keeping this in mind will also assist you with the inclusion of blueberries in red meat and salad dishes as mentioned above.

> *Dear Chef Dez:*
>
> *I love buying blueberries from our local farms in large quantities at a great price. What is the best way to freeze them? How long should I keep them before using them up?*
>
> *Joseph C.*
> *Mission, BC*

> *Dear Joseph:*
>
> *Blueberries are best frozen individually to make it easier to retrieve a certain measurement when they are frozen, rather than defrosting a solid mass of them. I find the best way to do this in sealable freezer bags. To make it easier to use them direct from their frozen state, I suggest washing them prior to freezing, however they would also need to be dried before going into the bag as wet berries will freeze to each other. I suggest keeping frozen blueberries for up to a year for best results.*

# BC Birthday Cobb Salad

**Full colour photo available at www.chefdez.com**

*"To celebrate BC's 150th Birthday, I wrote this version of cob salad with ingredients that are the same colours as our BC flag – Blue, Red, Yellow, and White."*

<u>Dressing Ingredients</u>
5 strips of bacon
1 clove of garlic
¼ (one quarter) cup red wine vinegar
1 tbsp lemon juice
1 tbsp sugar
1 tsp Worcestershire sauce
1 tsp salt
½ (one half) tsp pepper
¼ (one quarter) tsp dry mustard
½ (one half) cup extra virgin olive oil

1.  Cook the bacon in a frying pan until crisp. Reserve the rendered fat.
2.  Place the bacon strips and the garlic in a food processor and process until minced.
3.  Add the reserved bacon fat to the food processor along with all of the remaining ingredients, except for the extra virgin olive oil. Puree on high speed.
4.  With the food processor still on high speed, slowly add the olive oil until thoroughly combined. Makes approximately 1 cup of dressing.

<u>Salad Ingredients</u>
2 large romaine hearts
2 cups (1 pint) fresh blueberries
3 hard boiled eggs, peeled, quartered, and cut into small chunks
1 cup quartered cherry tomatoes
1 cup crumbled mild blue cheese (suggestion: Danish Blue Rosenborg)
~or~ 1 cup crumbled feta cheese if you don't care for blue cheese
1 cup drained canned corn kernels
1 red bell pepper, cut into thin 1-inch strips, approx. 1 cup

1. Cut the romaine hearts into small bite size pieces. Wash thoroughly and spin dry in a salad spinner. If the romaine is too wet it will water-down the taste of the dressing. Place on a large deep serving platter that will be big enough for tossing before serving. The romaine should be placed evenly across the platter (not mounded up).

2. By the time you have finished assembling the salad, you should have seven equal strips of ingredients covering the romaine lettuce. Start with first putting two strips of blueberries (1 cup for each strip) on each end of the pile of lettuce.

3. Then working left to right (from one strip of blueberries to the other) place the remaining ingredients in equal sized strips on the romaine lettuce: eggs, tomatoes, blue cheese, corn, and red pepper. You are now finished assembling the salad and the romain lettuce should be completely covered with seven strips of ingredients that are the same colour as the BC Flag. Bring to the table to display with the vinaigrette separate.

4. Just before serving, pour the dressing over the salad and toss thoroughly.

*Serves 4 as a meal, or 6 to 8 as a side dish*

# Blueberry BBQ Sauce

*"A fantastic grilling sauce made from fresh or frozen blueberries. Tastes great on chicken, pork or beef!"*

3 cups blueberries
3 garlic cloves, minced or pressed
¼ (one quarter) cup dark brown sugar
¼ (one quarter) cup minced onion
¼ (one quarter) cup ketchup
¼ (one quarter) cup white vinegar
¼ (one quarter) cup molasses
2 tsp salt
½ (one half) tsp pepper

1. Add all ingredients to a medium heavy bottomed pot.
2. Turn heat to medium and bring to a boil while mashing the blueberries with a potato masher.

3.  Once boiling, turn heat to low and simmer uncovered for 5 minutes.
4.  Transfer to a blender and puree smooth. Most blenders can handle hot liquids but if you are unsure if yours can or not, let the sauce cool first before pureeing. Always be careful when handling hot liquids – make sure the lid of your blender is on tight and to be safe hold the lid down with a towel or oven mitt to protect your hand.

*Makes approximately 2.5 cups*

# Blueberry Bread Pudding

1 – 454g (1 pound) French loaf
4 large eggs, beaten
1.25 cups sugar
1 tsp vanilla extract
1 tsp ground cinnamon
¼ (one quarter) tsp salt
Zest from 2 lemons, finely chopped
2 cups 10%MF cream (half and half)
2 cups milk (2%MF or 3.5%Homogenized)
1.5 to 2 cups blueberries (fresh or thawed frozen)
Vanilla bean ice cream, optional

1.  Preheat oven to 400 degrees. Tear the French bread into approximate 1 inch to 2 inch chunks and spread evenly on a large baking sheet. Bake in the oven for 10 minutes, tossing the pieces around about halfway through. Remove from the oven and let sit while you prepare the rest of the pudding.
2.  Decrease the oven temperature to 350 degrees and prepare a 9x13 baking dish by buttering it.
3.  In a large bowl, combine the eggs, sugar, vanilla, cinnamon, salt, and the zest thoroughly. Whisk in the cream and milk. Add the toasted bread

pieces and toss together thoroughly with your hands. Let sit for 10 minutes for the bread pieces to absorb.

4. Put one half of the custard soaked bread mixture into the prepared baking dish and top with half of the blueberries. Add the remaining bread mixture (and scrape all liquid from the bowl) to the dish and top with the remaining blueberries. Bake for approximately 1 hour until the top browns and puffs up. Also an inserted butter knife should come out clean.

5. Let sit for at least 10 to 15 minutes before serving warm with vanilla bean ice cream.

*Makes 10 to 12 portions*

# Blueberry Salsa

**Full colour photo available at www.chefdez.com**

*"The contrast of the fresh blueberries with the other ingredients is absolutely mouthwatering"*

1 medium yellow bell pepper diced small
½ (one half) jalapeno, minced – seeds & membrane removed for a milder salsa
¼ (one quarter) cup small diced red onion
2 – 4 tbsp finely chopped fresh mint
Zest from 1 lime, finely chopped
2 tbsp lime juice
1 tsp sugar
1 tsp fresh cracked black pepper
¼ (one quarter) tsp salt
1 ½ (one and one half) cups fresh blueberries

1. Mix all of the ingredients together, except for the blueberries.
2. Gently toss in the fresh blueberries into the salsa ingredients.
3. Serve the salsa over the grilled chicken or fish.

*Makes approximately 2 cups*

# Grilled Blueberry Brie Chicken Sandwich

**Full colour photo available at www.chefdez.com**

*"The balance between the sweet blueberries and blueberry syrup with the pungent creaminess of the garlic cream cheese is incredible when paired with the grilled chicken and melted brie cheese. I know that the inclusion of blueberries and syrup in a chicken sandwich sounds odd, but you need to try this – your taste buds will thank you!"*

½ (one half) 250g tub of spreadable cream cheese
1 large garlic clove, crushed
4 chicken breast halves, cut butterflied to make them thinner
3 tbsp olive oil
Salt & pepper
1 – 454g flat ciabatta bread loaf
100g brie cheese, sliced thin
4 tbsp blueberry syrup
1 1/3 (one and one third) cups fresh blueberries (approximately)

1. Preheat grill over high heat.
2. Place the 125g cream cheese in a small mixing bowl and combine with the garlic and ¼ (one quarter) teaspoon of salt.
3. Oil the chicken with 1 tbsp of the olive oil and season with salt and pepper.
4. Grill the chicken over medium heat/flame until cooked through, flipping only once, approximately 2 to 4 minutes per side depending on the thickness and temperature of the chicken.
5. Cut the ciabatta loaf into four equal pieces and then cut each of the four pieces in half horizontally to create a sandwich top and bottom with each one. Brush the other 2 tbsp of olive oil over the cut sides of the bread and grill cut/oiled side down until lightly toasted.
6. When the chicken is almost cooked, distribute the brie slices evenly over the chicken and close the lid on the BBQ to melt the cheese, approximately 1 to 2 minutes. ~ Or ~ alternatively once the chicken is cooked distribute the brie slices evenly over the chicken and broil in the oven until cheese is melted.
7. Assemble each of the four sandwiches as follows: On the bottom half of each sandwich, drizzle 1 tbsp blueberry syrup and place the chicken/brie

on top of it. On the top half of each sandwich spread ¼ (one quarter) of the garlic cream cheese mixture and 1/3 (one third) cup of fresh blueberries gently pressed into the surface of the garlic cream cheese.

8. Serve open faced to display the blueberries and the melted brie on the chicken.

*Makes 4 sandwiches*

# Grilled Vegetable Salad with Blueberry Vinaigrette

*"Complex flavour is created by charring vegetables on the BBQ and the blueberries add a complimenting balance of sweetness to the dressing"*

## Vinaigrette Ingredients
1 ½ (one and one half) cups blueberries
¼ (one quarter) cup balsamic vinegar
1 garlic clove
1 tbsp lemon juice
1 tsp salt
½ (one half) tsp pepper
½ (one half) cup extra virgin olive oil

1. Place all the ingredients, except for the olive oil, in a food processor. Puree on high speed until thoroughly combined.
2. Add the olive oil slowly while the processor is still running. Makes approximately one and a half cups of dressing.

## Grilled Vegetable Salad Ingredients
1 large romaine heart
3 ears of corn, peeled
3 small-medium green zucchini, sliced thin lengthwise
2 large red bell peppers, quartered, seeds removed
1 large red onion, sliced thick
3 to 4 tbsp olive oil

Salt & pepper

2 to 3 tbsp sunflower seeds

1. Cut the romaine heart into small bite size pieces. Wash thoroughly and spin dry in a salad spinner. If the romaine is too wet it will water-down the taste of the dressing. Place in a large deep bowl that will be big enough for tossing with all of the grilled vegetables.
2. Preheat your grill over high heat.
3. Toss the corn, zucchini slices, red pepper pieces, and red onion slices with the olive oil and season with salt and pepper.
4. Place the vegetables on the grill and cook until all are starting to char.
5. Remove the vegetables from the grill. Remove the kernels of the corn by standing the ears upright and running a knife down the cob. Cut the remaining grilled vegetables into small half inch pieces.
6. Add all of the cut grilled vegetables to the cut romaine and toss with the vinaigrette. Garnish with the sunflower seeds and serve immediately.

*Serves approximately 10 – 12 people as a side dish, or 4 to 6 as a meal.*

# Mozza Stuffed Blueberry Hamburgers

*"A blueberry version of my popular hamburgers from the Father's Day chapter in this book. You have to try this to believe it!"*

1 kg lean ground beef

8 garlic cloves, crushed

1 egg

1 cup fresh blueberries

2/3 cup cornflake crumbs

½ (one half) cup minced onion

½ (one half) cup oil packed sundried tomatoes, drained & chopped

2 tbsp sugar

1 tbsp salt

1 tbsp dried basil leaves

1 tsp dried thyme leaves

1 tsp chilli powder

1 tsp pepper

100g mozzarella cheese, cut into 8 small chunks

1. Mix all of the ingredients together (except for the mozzarella) in a large bowl. While mixing, make an effort to crush the blueberries.
2. Preheat your cooking surface; pan, grill, griddle, etc.
3. Portion the hamburger mixture into eight equal sized balls.
4. Flatten each ball in your hand and encase a chunk of mozzarella in the middle by shaping it into a large patty, by wrapping the meat around the cheese.
5. Over a medium heat/flame, cook the patties until thoroughly cooked through, approximately 8 to 12 minutes per side.

*Ground hamburger patties must be completely cooked through to be safely consumed.

*Makes 8 large patties*

# Rack of Lamb with Blueberry Reduction

*"A reduction sauce made from blueberries! It is important for the pan to be hot enough to sear the racks – this will add flavour to both the meat and the sauce."*

2 racks of lamb approximately three-quarters of a pound each, frenched

2tbsp canola oil

Salt and freshly cracked pepper to taste

½ (one half) cup & a splash of red wine

2 cups blueberries

2 ½ (two and one half) tsp white sugar

2 tsp beef stock paste

2-3 tbsp whipping cream

1. Oil the lamb racks with one tablespoon of the oil, and season them with salt and pepper.
2. Preheat oven to 450 degrees.
3. Heat a heavy bottomed pan over medium heat.

4.  Add the other tablespoon of oil to the pan and sear the racks on both sides and ends. Approximately five minutes total.

5.  Place the racks in a pan on a wire rack and roast in oven for fifteen minutes (approximately medium rare).

6.  Deglaze the pan (remove the brown bits from the pan into the wine) with the splash of red wine, scraping with a wooden spoon.

7.  Add the other one half cup of red wine, berries, sugar, and beef paste to the pan, and bring to a boil over medium high heat.

8.  Reduce over the same temperature, while breaking up the berries with a spoon as they start to break down, approximately ten minutes. Mash the berries with a potato masher at this point.

9.  Strain this sauce through a wire mesh strainer and return the sauce to the pan. Discard the pulp left in the strainer.

10. Add the cream and reduce the sauce until it is thick and syrupy.

11. Remove the sauce from the heat, and transfer the sauce to a different container and cover to prevent evaporation while waiting for the lamb to be cooked.

12. Remove the lamb racks from the oven and let rest for five minutes to allow meat to retain its juices. Plate by either leaving them whole or by cutting each chop individually.

13. Drizzle the sauce on and around the lamb.

*Makes 2 - 4 servings*

# 13

## Butter. What do You Spread on Your Toast?

When it comes to cooking, baking, and mealtime, butter has a definite role in the kitchen and at the dinner table. I know that even mentioning the comparison of butter to margarine is going to stir up a lot of opinions, but even with my expectation of receiving negative emails I am going to express my view.

We use butter in our home on a daily basis for cooking, baking and serving and I cannot even remember the last time margarine made its way into my refrigerator. In my opinion nothing is better for flavour, richness, melt ability, texture, and in moderation, health benefits.

Butter is one of the oldest and most natural products there is, yet it has taken quite a beating by margarines. Many people buy margarine due to budgetary restrictions, but I would assume that there are just as many, if not more, that purchase it because of perceived health benefits. Not all margarines are created equal and it is important to read the labels of any product that is manufactured and/or processed, including butter.

If one is purchasing margarine, one of the main things to look out for in an ingredient list is "hydrogenated" oil. Hydrogenation is the process used to transform liquid oil into a solid fat at room temperature. Vegetable shortening, many peanut butters and various margarines are made in this manner and this process creates <u>artificially produced</u> trans fats which are now considered the worst type of fat for the heart. Butter is not processed using hydrogenation. As a matter of fact, butter is hardly processed at all. What butter does have is a very small amount of <u>naturally occurring</u> trans fat, also present in the meat of animals such as beef and lamb.

A 1994 Harvard University study, as well as research from other credible sources, have concluded that a diet high in Trans Fat doubles the chance for heart attack and decreases life expectancy. While trans fats can occur naturally, they are most commonly associated with chemical preservative techniques like hydrogenation and health experts recommend that you limit your intake of hydrogenated or partially-hydrogenated foodstuffs as much as possible.

It is also important to point out that a two teaspoon serving of butter has no more calories or fat than margarine or olive oil.

So are butter, margarine, and vegetable oils bad for you? First of all, let's point out that the term "bad" is not very definitive. It depends on what you are looking for and it is imperative to keep in mind that there are pros and cons for everything. Let's face it; no matter what type of fat you are ingesting on a regular basis, moderation is the key, as with almost everything. For instance, many doctors may tell you that red wine is good for you, but always in moderation: One glass per day may be fine, but two or three glasses per day not so much.

No matter how you look at it, nothing can replace the flavour and mouth feel of butter, and also the texture created by using it in baked goods.

> *Dear Chef Dez:*
> *Some recipes call for unsalted butter and also call for salt. Please explain why this is?*
>
> *Vivian D.*
> *Surrey, BC*

> *Dear Vivian:*
> *Usually one will often see this by pastry chefs wanting to control the amount of salt in their pastry, which is usually less than the percentage found in the butter.*
> *Unless making very precise recipes, there is no need to use unsalted butter and I have always used salted butter for everything. It is less expensive than unsalted butter and butter is expensive enough already.*

# Beurre Blanc

*"Beurre Blanc is a French term for White Butter Sauce. Excellent on fish or vegetables!*

2 shallots, minced
¼ (one quarter) cup white wine
2 tbsp white wine vinegar
½ (one half) cup cold butter, cubed into small pieces
Salt & fresh cracked pepper, to taste

1. Add shallots, wine and vinegar to a medium size pan and place over high heat. Bring to a boil and reduce the liquid in the pan to one tablespoon.
2. Reduce the heat to very low and start whisking the mixture while adding the cold butter pieces one at a time. Make sure that the butter is melting slowly so you can whisk it into a sauce consistency – if it melts too quickly it will just be a greasy mess. If it is melting too quickly, remove the pan from the heat for a minute or two and whisk it constantly before returning it to the low heat to continue whisking in the remaining butter.
3. When all the butter has been incorporated, season to taste with salt & pepper and serve immediately.

# Homemade Butter

*"Kids love making this recipe"*

1 cup cold whipping cream
1 lidded jar, that holds at least 2 cups
Salt to taste – starting with 1/8 teaspoon (one pinch)

2 or 3 children with some energy to burn off

1. Pour the cream into the jar and seal tightly with the lid.
2. Shake vigorously for approximately 15 to 20 minutes, until a solid (butter) and a watery liquid (buttermilk) forms.

3. Strain the liquids from the butter with a wire-mesh strainer.
4. Transfer the butter to a bowl and mix the salt into it.

*Makes approximately one half cup of butter*

# Pan Seared Scallops with Sage Brown Butter Sauce

**Full colour photo available at www.chefdez.com**

*"The essential oils released from the fresh sage in this sauce make these scallops to die for"*

12 medium scallops
Salt & Pepper
1 – 2 tsp grape-seed oil or canola oil
1/3 (one third) cup cold butter, cubed into tbsp pieces
2 tbsp chopped fresh sage

1. Preheat a heavy bottomed medium/large pan over medium-high heat until it is very hot.
2. Pat dry the scallops and season them on both sides with salt & pepper.
3. Add the oil and then immediately add the scallops one or two at a time. Cook in the hot pan for about 30 seconds to a minute on the one side until they are seared.
4. Flip them over, cook for another 30 seconds, then add the butter pieces one or two at a time until it has all been added. The butter will brown very quickly and immediately add the sage, stir and coat the scallops with the infused brown butter sauce and serve immediately.

# Pasta with Butter, Garlic, & Cheese

*"Probably one of the simplest side pasta dishes"*

1/3 (one third) cup butter
3 to 4 garlic cloves, crushed
250g dry linguine
½ (one half) cup grated parmesan or romano cheese
Salt & fresh cracked pepper
1 small handful of parsley, chopped fine

1. Place a large non-stick pan over low heat. Add the butter and the crushed garlic cloves. Let the butter melt and get infused with the garlic. Do not increase the temperature of the pan to ensure not burning the garlic or butter. Put a large pot of salted water on high heat to bring to a boil in the meantime.
2. Once the water is boiling cook the dry linguine for approximately 8 minutes, or until desired consistency is reached.
3. Drain the cooked pasta and shake thoroughly to rid it of as much excess water as possible. Add to the melted butter and toss with the cheese.
4. Season to taste with salt and fresh cracked pepper and garnish with the chopped parsley.

*Makes 4 to 6 side portions*

# Patricia's Mediterranean Chicken

**Full colour photo available at www.chefdez.com**

*"I wrote this recipe for country artist Patricia Conroy. Goat cheese covered grilled chicken topped with a sundried tomato & artichoke sauce infused with garlic, white wine, fresh lemon juice and basil. Very rich and very delicious."*

6 boneless, skinless chicken breast halves
Olive oil
Salt & pepper

2 tbsp butter

3 to 4 garlic cloves, minced

2 tbsp minced onion

½ (one half) cup dry white wine

Juice from 2 lemons (approx. one quarter cup), zest reserved

1 cup chopped oil packed sundried tomatoes, drained

1 – 398ml/14 oz. can artichoke hearts, drained and quartered

¼ (one quarter) cup whipping cream

2 tsp sugar

½ (one half) tsp salt

½ (one half) tsp pepper

2/3 (two thirds) cup cold butter, cut in small pieces

¼ (one quarter) cup chopped fresh basil

227g soft unripened goat cheese

1. Brush the chicken breasts with olive oil and season with salt and pepper. Grill over a medium flame for approximately 15 to 20 minutes until cooked through.

2. While chicken is cooking prepare the sauce. Melt the 2 tbsp butter in a pan over medium heat. Add the garlic and onion and sauté until soft, approximately 2 to 3 minutes.

3. Stir in the wine and lemon juice, increase heat to medium high and reduce until half of the liquid has evaporated, approximately 3 to 5 minutes.

4. Stir in the tomatoes, artichokes, cream, sugar, salt and pepper.

5. Turn off the heat. Add the butter one piece at a time while stirring to incorporate. Once all the butter has been added, stir in the basil.

6. Divide the goat cheese into 6 equal portions. During the last 2 minutes of cooking time for the chicken, top with the goat cheese.

7. Serve the cheese topped chicken immediately with the sauce spooned over top.

8. Garnish with the reserved lemon zest.

*Makes 6 portions*

# 14

## Flour Power

Not only is flour considered the most beneficial ingredient in baking, but also it is an ingredient found in almost every household kitchen. Therefore the more one knows about this necessity, the better the judgments made in refining culinary adventures.

Although there are a number of varieties of flour available, the majority of them are made from wheat. This will be my focus for the rationale of this column. The main varieties of wheat flour available will vary slightly from store to store, but will typically be all-purpose, cake & pastry, and bread flour.

Wheat produced into flour can be separated into two categories: hard or soft kernel. The milling process begins at separating the bran, germ, and endosperm of these wheat categories. It is from the endosperm that flour, as we know it, is created as it is milled into a powder. Whole-wheat flours, on the other hand, are made from milling together all three components of the wheat kernel, not just the endosperm.

The flour from hard wheat contains a higher gluten content than soft wheat. Higher gluten is beneficial to creating structure in baked goods, such as breads and pizza crusts. When flour is mixed with a liquid, the gluten is responsible for the elastic responsiveness of dough.

Cake & pastry flour is made entirely from soft wheat to provide a low gluten content to ensure the tenderness of these delicate goods. This flour is therefore generally used with leaveners such as baking powder, baking soda, and/or eggs, and then keeping agitation/mixing to a minimum.

Bread flour is made entirely from hard wheat to provide a high gluten content to ensure texture in breads. Yeast is almost always the leavener with bread flour. The elastic strands of dough capture yeast gases as it bakes, giving the bread height and structure.

All-purpose flour is a mixture of both hard and soft wheat, and functions in the manner that the name represents. It is good for all applications such as breads, cakes or pastries, but it is not ideal.

Superior quality baked goods will always start from the correct selection of flour.

> Dear Chef Dez:
>
> In a previous column about quick breads, you wrote that gluten is formed/created when flour is mixed together with a liquid. However, you also mentioned that bread flour "contains" more gluten than all-purpose or pastry flour.
>
> What is the difference between the gluten that is already present in flour, and the gluten that is formed when flour is mixed with a liquid?
>
> Gerrit B.
> Maple Ridge, BC

> Dear Gerrit:
>
> This is a very excellent question. The terms are basically synonymous with each other. Let me see if I can try to make it easy to understand.
>
> If the term "gluten" is referred to, when discussing raw flours, it is in reference to the amount of hard wheat content in the flour. This is in turn responsible for the amount of "gluten" created when moisture is added and agitated. One will say, "create gluten" when mixing, but more accurately it would be described as "making it more apparent" by the kneading/mixing process. This in turn makes the gluten (the one in the raw flour) stringy and stretchy - giving us structure in baked goods such as bread.

# Apple Cinnamon Bran Muffins

1 cup whole wheat flour
1 cup bran flakes cereal, lightly compacted
2 tsp baking powder
1 tsp cinnamon
½ (one half) tsp salt
1 cup apple - peeled & diced ½ inch
½ (one half) cup Splenda granulated sweetener
¼ (one quarter) cup butter, room temperature
¼ (one quarter) cup buttermilk
¼ (one quarter) cup unsweetened apple sauce
2 eggs
More ground cinnamon for sprinkling

1. Preheat oven to 400 degrees and prepare a 12 cup muffin tin with baking spray.
2. Combine the whole wheat flour, bran flakes cereal, baking powder, ground cinnamon, and salt in a mixing bowl.
3. Toss the diced apples into this dry mixture.
4. Beat the Splenda and butter together in a separate bowl.
5. Add the buttermilk, apple sauce, and eggs to the butter and Splenda mixture. Continue beating until thoroughly combined.
6. Combine the mixtures in the two bowls together to form a batter.
7. Spoon the mixture evenly into the prepared muffin tin. Approximately two thirds full in each.
8. Sprinkle a small amount of cinnamon on each muffin.
9. Bake for 15 minutes and cool in the pan before serving.

*Makes small 12 muffins*

# Cheddar Sesame Crackers

Recipe created by Katherine Desormeaux (Mrs. Chef Dez)

2 cups whole wheat flour
2 cups grated old cheddar cheese
3 tablespoons sugar
1 teaspoon salt
¼ (one quarter) tsp paprika
¼ (one quarter) tsp ground cayenne (optional)
½ (one half) cup butter, frozen
½ (one half) cup water
Extra whole wheat flour for rolling
¼ (one quarter) to 1/3 (one third) cup sesame seeds

1. Preheat your oven to 425 degrees Fahrenheit.
2. Mix the flour, cheddar, sugar, salt, paprika, cayenne together in a bowl. Using a standard cheese grater, grate the frozen butter into this dry mixture and toss to mix. Add the water and mix until just combined to form a dough. Cut the dough into four equal parts.
3. Flatten out one portion of dough in your hands and sprinkle a small amount of flour on the counter and on top of the portion of the dough. Start rolling out the dough while ensuring the underside stays well floured. When the top of the dough starts to stick to the rolling pin sprinkle it with a generous amount of sesame seeds and roll the seeds onto the dough until it is approximately 1/8th of an inch thick. Note: if you use too much flour on the top of the dough, the sesame seeds will not stick; the seeds will help to keep the dough from sticking to the rolling pin. Cut the rolled dough into desired shapes and place on an ungreased baking sheet. Bake for approximately 5 to 6 minutes or until they have just turned brown. Because of the cheddar cheese and sesame seeds they must be watched closely to ensure they don't burn. Remove from the baking sheet to cool on a wire rack. Repeat with the other 3 portions of dough.
4. When completely cooled, store in an air-tight container at room temperature for up to 5 days. Makes approximately 4 to 5 dozen depending on how small you cut the shapes.

# Oatmeal Breakfast Bars

**Full colour photo available at www.chefdez.com**

*"The benefit of oatmeal in a convenient bar. Great for Breakfast on the run too – Microwave each bar from frozen for 30 seconds on high power."*

2 ¼ (two and a quarter) cups whole wheat flour
2 ¼ (two and a quarter) cups quick oats
¾ (three quarters) cup raisins
3 tbsp ground flax seed
1½ (one and one half) tsp baking soda
1½ (one and one half) tsp cinnamon
1 tsp salt
¾ (three quarters) cup butter, room temperature
½ (one half) cup Splenda Brown Sugar Blend
1 cup unsweetened apple sauce
1½ (one and one half) tsp vanilla extract
2 eggs

1. Preheat oven to 350 degrees and prepare a 9 x 13 inch cake pan with baking spray. Tip: Line the pan with parchment paper leaving the ends sticking out to make the uncut product easier to remove from the pan once cooled.
2. Combine the whole wheat flour, quick oats, raisins, ground flax seed, baking soda, ground cinnamon, and salt in a mixing bowl.
3. Beat the butter and Splenda Brown Sugar Blend together in a separate bowl.
4. Add the apple sauce, vanilla extract and eggs to the butter and Splenda/butter mixture. Continue beating until thoroughly combined.
5. Combine the mixtures in the two bowls together. It will be a very thick batter.
6. Press the mixture evenly into the prepared pan.
7. Bake for 18-20 minutes until firm.
8. Cool in the pan until room temperature.
9. Cut into 16 equal bars by removing the product from the pan first.

*Makes 16 bars*

# Pizza Crust Dough

*"Grilling the pizza crust on the barbeque gives it a flame licked taste that is reminiscent of cooking it in a wood fired forno oven"*

2½ (two and one half) cups all-purpose flour
2 tsp instant yeast
2 tsp sugar
¾ (three quarters) tsp salt
¾ (three quarters) cup + 2 tbsp water, room temperature
2 tbsp extra-virgin olive oil

1. Mix the flour, yeast, sugar, and salt in a large bowl. Add the water & olive oil and mix until it starts coming together. Turn out onto a lightly floured surface and knead for 7-8 minutes until smooth and elastic.

2. Place the dough in a lightly oiled bowl, cover with plastic wrap, and let sit for approximately one hour until doubled in volume. Make sure this is done in a warm place with no drafts. While the dough is proofing, prepare your desired sauce and toppings.

3. Alternatively, you can use a bread-maker by putting in all of the crust ingredients and selecting the 'dough' setting.

4. Punch down the dough. Remove from the bowl and divide into four equal portions. Roll out each portion into a roughly shaped 8 to 10 inch circle.

5. Preheat grill over medium-high heat.

6. Place one pizza dough round on the grill and lower the heat to medium. Cook the one side for approximately 5 minutes until golden brown and lightly charred (while gently piercing any air bubbles with a fork).

7. Flip the crust over and turn off the grill while you assemble your pizza toppings on the cooked side of the crust. Once assembled, turn your grill back on and cook the bottom side of the crust for approximately 2 to 3 more minutes until that side is golden brown as well.

*Makes 4, eight to ten inch pizzas*

# Scottish Dundee Cake with Scotch Infused Whip Cream

**Full colour photo available at www.chefdez.com**

*"A famous traditional Scottish fruit cake with rich flavour and texture"*

1 ¼ (one and one quarter) cups sultanas
2/3 (two thirds) cup currants
½ (one half) cup dark raisins
¼ (one quarter) cup chopped mixed peel
Zest from 1 lemon, chopped
Zest from 1 large orange, chopped
¼ (one quarter) cup Scotch whiskey
¾ (three quarters) cup butter, room temperature
1/3 (one third) cup dark brown sugar
1/3 (one third) cup white granulated sugar
3 large eggs
1/3 (one third) cup milk
1 ½ (one and one half) cups flour
1 tsp baking powder
2 tbsp ground almonds
½ (one half) tsp salt
20 whole blanched almonds

1.   Preheat oven to 325 degrees. Prepare a 9-inch round cake pan with baking spray (and with parchment paper if desired).
2.   Combine sultanas, currants, raisins, peel, zests, and whiskey together in a mixing bowl.
3.   In a separate bowl beat the butter with the two sugars, scraping down the sides as necessary. Gradually add each egg and continue beating until fully combined. Add this mixture and the milk to the fruit/whiskey mixture and combine thoroughly.
4.   In a separate bowl combine all the dry ingredients: Flour, baking powder, ground almonds, and salt. Add this into the other mixture and fold to combine.
5.   Spread mixture evenly into prepared pan and top decoratively with the almonds.

6.  Bake for approximately 1 hour or until a tooth pick inserted comes out clean. Let cool in the pan on a rack for at least 20 minutes. Cut and serve with Scotch infused whip cream.

250ml whipping cream
1 tbsp white granulated sugar
1 tbsp Scotch whiskey

1.  On high speed beat the cream and the sugar together. When it just starts to get thick, add the whiskey and continue beating until fully whipped.

*Makes one 9-inch cake*

# The World's Best Cornbread
**Full colour photo available at www.chefdez.com**
*"In my opinion, I am sure you have never tasted cornbread better than this!"*

1 cup yellow cornmeal
½ (one half) cup all purpose flour
1 tsp baking powder
¼ (one quarter) tsp baking soda
2 tbsp white sugar
1 cup grated cheddar cheese
1 cup frozen corn kernels
½ (one half) jalapeno pepper, diced small
¼ (one quarter) red bell pepper, diced small
½ (one half) tsp salt
2 eggs, beaten
½ (one half) cup sour cream
½ (one half) cup milk
¼ (one quarter) cup vegetable oil

1. Preheat the oven to 400 degrees and spray an 8 inch square pan with baking spray.
2. Place the cornmeal, flour, baking powder, baking soda, sugar, cheese, corn, jalapeno, bell pepper, and salt in a large bowl – mix to combine.
3. Place the eggs, sour cream, milk, and oil in a second bowl – mix to combine.
4. Add the wet ingredients to the dry ingredients, and mix until just combined. Pour into the prepared 8 inch pan and bake for approximately 30 minutes until golden brown and an inserted toothpick comes out clean.
5. Cut the cornbread into 4 or 6 equal portions.

*Makes 4 or 6 servings*

# 15

## *Reduce Liquids to Increase Flavours*

Have you ever experienced an incredible meal at a fine dining establishment, which included an intensely flavoured accompanying sauce? Chances are you have. These companion sauces, although sparse in volume on the plate, deliver unmistakable and compelling tastes reminiscent of the flavours in the food being served. With the knowledge of some sauce basics and some practiced perfection, anyone can accomplish this same feat in their home kitchen.

Long gone are the days that described gourmet cooking as dishes covered in thick glutinous sauces. In today's culinary world, our aspirations are to enhance food with sauces that are created from naturally occurring liquids in the recipe without a starch thickener. An accompanying sauce should be that: to accompany, not govern, the food.

Reduction sauces are thickened naturally by evaporation. Creating steam is the action of transforming water into vapour. When a sauce is simmering in a pan, and steam is rising from the pan, it is accurate to assume then, that the sauce is concentrating. Water alone has no flavour, so as it evaporates from the recipe, residual flavours left in the pan are intensified.

Not only does this affect taste, but texture as well. With the evaporation of water content the sauce also becomes less pliable or more accurately stated, syrupy. This is vital for creating a sauce with texture and visual appeal as it coats the food being served.

An example of this technique would be a wine reduction sauce served with pan-seared steaks. Sear the steaks in a heavy-bottomed stainless steel pan until the desired doneness is achieved. Remove the steaks from the pan and keep warm while the sauce is prepared. Add one half cup or more of full bodied red wine to deglaze the pan (removing the browned bits of flavour left on the pan from searing the steaks) with the help of a wooden spoon. Add some beef broth, a bit of sugar (to counteract acidity in the wine), and boil over medium to medium-high heat (stirring constantly) until the desired consistency is reached. Add a bit of whipping cream for richness, season to taste with salt & pepper, and reduce until syrupy. Take the pan off the heat and melt a teaspoon of butter into the sauce to give it a glistening appearance. Serve immediately over the steaks.

In this example, the flavour of the steak remnants is incorporated into the wine. The wine and broth are reduced to eliminate their water content to increase flavour intensity and sauce density. Flavourings are added along with some richness from the addition of cream and butter to complete the sauce.

There are many other flavours you can add to create incredible sauces you can call your own. Look at recipes and change them based on your taste preferences. Be creative in your kitchen and experiment with this process. With perseverance, I am sure you will be making restaurant quality sauce reductions in a very short time.

Dear Chef Dez:
I tried making a beef stew without following a recipe, and it turned out bland and watery. What is the most important thing you can recommend to help me?
Rob M.
Burnaby, BC

Dear Rob.
Other than Browning the beef and making sure you have a good assortment of ingredients to provide a complex taste, I would recommend not adding any water. Water has no flavour and there are so many choices of liquids to add to recipes that do. Depending on what type of dish you are making, I would add wine, beer, broth, or juice instead of water. When water reduces you are left with nothing, but when one of these alternatives are reduced you are left with intensified flavour.

# Kristal's Sweet Chili Lime Seafood Medley

**Full colour photo available at www.chefdez.com**

*"I wrote this recipe for country artist Kristal Barrett. The sauce is easily transformed into a complex syrupy reduction by using the same red pepper jelly that one would normally serve with cheese and crackers. The final product is sweet but also bursting with fresh lime flavor with just a touch of heat from the pepper jelly. The vegetables can be served separately (as pictured) or underneath the seafood for a beautiful display"*

### Vegetables

1 small green zucchini, sliced into thin strips
1 large red bell pepper, sliced into thin strips
1 large yellow bell pepper, sliced into thin strips
1 tbsp thinly sliced fresh ginger
1 garlic clove, thinly sliced
1 tbsp olive oil
Salt & pepper

1. Heat a large pan over medium-high heat.
2. Add the olive oil and then all the vegetables. Season with salt and pepper and cook until just soft, tossing frequently, approximately 5 to 7 minutes.
3. Taste and re-season with more salt and pepper if necessary.
4. Remove from heat and set aside for plating.

### Sweet Chili Lime Seafood

1 tbsp olive oil
340g (0.75 lb) raw large tiger prawns, peeled & deveined
12 large raw scallops
1/3 (one third) cup white wine
Juice of 2 limes (zest removed first and reserved for garnish)
½ (one half) cup prepared red pepper jelly
½ (one half) tsp salt

1. Heat a separate large nonstick pan over medium-high heat.
2. Add the olive oil. Add the scallops and let them sear on one side for approximately 30 seconds to 1 minute.

3. Turn the scallops over and sear the other side for another 30 seconds to 1 minute.

4. Slowly add the wine, then add the lime juice, pepper jelly and salt. Stir until the pepper jelly has melted into the liquid.

5. Once the liquid is boiling, add the prawns and cook, while stirring frequently, until the prawns have just turned pink. (Overcooked prawns become rubbery)

6. Immediately remove the scallops and prawns from the pan and set aside.

7. Turn the heat to high and boil (reduce) the sauce until syrupy enough to coat a spoon. *Hint – you will need to remove than pan from the heat to the let boiling subside in order to see how syrupy the sauce is getting.

8. Quickly toss the seafood into this reduction to coat. Do not add any of the liquid that may have come out of the seafood while it was set aside – this will only thin out the sauce.

9. Plate each portion with a mound of the sautéed vegetables, three scallops, and equal amounts of prawns. Drizzle the sauce reduction over the seafood, garnish with the reserved lime zest and serve immediately.

*Makes 4 portions*

# Merlot Sauced Steak Sandwich

**Full colour photo available at www.chefdez.com**

*"A unique flavourful steak sandwich served open-faced on naan bread"*

1 cup & 2 tbsp merlot or other full bodied red wine
1 med – large shallot, minced
1 garlic clove, minced
1 bay leaf
½ (one half) tsp dried thyme leaves
½ (one half) tsp sugar
1 – 2 tsp cornstarch
Salt & pepper

Vegetable oil
2 thin "fast fry" prime rib steaks, bone removed
2 slices naan bread
1 - 2 tbsp butter mixed with 1 crushed garlic clove

1. In a heavy-bottomed small saucepan, put the 1 cup merlot, shallot, garlic, bay leaf, and thyme. Bring to a boil over med-high heat.
2. Lower the heat to medium and reduce until only just over a quarter cup remains in the saucepan.
3. Strain the solids from the liquid through a wire mesh strainer, and put the liquid back into the saucepan (discard the solids). Add the sugar and stir to dissolve.
4. In a small separate bowl, mix the cornstarch with the 2 tbsp of merlot.
5. Stir in a very small amount of the cornstarch mixture into the sauce, and bring the sauce to a boil over medium heat, stirring constantly. Continue to add just enough of the cornstarch mixture until the sauce looks like a glaze – not too thick!
6. Season to taste with salt & pepper and set the sauce aside.
7. Rub both sides of the steaks with a small amount of oil and season with salt and pepper.
8. Brush the naans with the garlic butter.
9. Sear the steaks in a hot pan or hot grill for approximately 1 to 1.5 minutes per side.
10. Warm the naans in the oven while the steaks are cooking.
11. For each person serve one naan, top it with a steak and drizzle with one half of the merlot sauce.

*Makes 2 open faced steak sandwiches*

# Pan Roasted Duck Breast with Red Wine Reduction

2 boneless duck breasts, skin on
Salt and pepper
½ (one half) tsp beef stock paste
½ (one half) to ¾ (three quarters) cup full bodied, dry, red wine
½ (one half) tsp sugar
2 - 3 tbsp heavy cream

1.  Score the skin (not the flesh underneath) of the duck breasts many times in two diagonal directions to create half-inch diamond shapes in the skin. Season both sides of the duck breasts with salt and pepper.
2.  Preheat the oven to 400 degrees.
3.  Place the seasoned, scored duck breasts, skin side down, in a cold oven-proof pan big enough to ensure there is space between the two breasts. Place the pan over medium heat and do not disturb the duck breasts except to spoon off the rendered fat from the skin. They will release from the pan once the skin has crisped in approximately 10 to 13 minutes. Keep spooning off the rendered fat into a separate dish during this process.
4.  Once the skin side has crisped, turn the heat to medium high and brown the flesh side of the duck breasts for approximately 1 minute.
5.  Place the pan in the preheated oven and cook until medium-rare (135-140 degrees internal temperature on the thickest part of the breast), approximately 7 to 8 minutes.
6.  Remove the breasts and side aside to rest for 8 to 10 minutes. Remove the residual fat from the pan.
7.  Let the pan cool a bit before adding the beef stock paste and then slowly adding the red wine to deglaze. Place the pan over medium-high heat (be careful of the hot handle from the oven) and add the sugar and cream. Stir constantly while reducing the sauce into a syrupy consistency and then transfer the sauce immediately to a separate container to prevent further evaporation from the hot pan.
8.  Serve the hot wine reduction with the rested duck breasts immediately.

*Makes 2 portions*

# Pork Medallions in Single Malt Pan Sauce

*"Live like the Scots – Scotch is not just for drinking, it's for cooking too!"*

1 - 500g pork tenderloin
2 tsp canola oil
Salt & pepper
½ (one half) cup chicken broth
¼ (one quarter) cup single malt Scotch
Juice of ½ (one half) lemon
1 tbsp liquid honey
¼ (one quarter) cup whipping cream

1. Cut the tenderloin into 12 equal sized medallions, approximately one half inch to three quarter inch thickness. Toss with the oil and season both sides with salt and pepper.
2. Heat a heavy bottomed pan over medium high heat.
3. When the pan is hot add the medallions and sear them for approximately 2 to 3 minutes on each side.
4. Add the chicken stock to the pan to deglaze (stir briefly to remove the browned bits off the pan into the sauce).
5. Add the Scotch carefully and ignite with a long match. Flambé until the flames subside.
6. Add the lemon juice, honey and cream. Continue to boil until syrupy and desired sauce consistency. Remove from heat, lightly season to taste with salt and pepper, and serve immediately.

*Makes 4 portions (3 medallions each)*

# Rack of Lamb with Blackberry Demiglaze

*"A sauce made from blackberries – you have to taste it to believe it! It is important for the pan to be hot enough to sear the racks – this will add flavour to both the meat and the sauce."*

2 racks of lamb approximately three-quarters of a pound each, frenched
2tbsp canola oil
Salt and freshly cracked pepper to taste
½ (one half) cup & a splash of red wine
2 cups frozen or fresh blackberries
2 ½ (two and one half) tsp white sugar
2 tsp beef stock paste
1 tsp butter

1.  Oil the lamb racks with one tablespoon of the oil, and season them with salt and pepper.
2.  Preheat oven to 450 degrees.
3.  Heat a heavy bottomed pan over medium heat.
4.  Add the other tablespoon of oil to the pan and sear the racks on both sides and ends. Approximately five minutes total.
5.  Place the racks in a pan on a wire rack and roast in oven for fifteen minutes (approximately medium rare).
6.  Deglaze the pan (remove the brown bits from the pan into the wine) with the splash of red wine, scraping with a wooden spoon.
7.  Add the other half cup of red wine, berries, sugar, and beef paste to the pan, and bring to a boil over medium high heat.
8.  Reduce over the same temperature, while breaking up the berries with a spoon as they start to break down, approximately ten minutes. Mash the berries with a potato masher at this point.
9.  Strain this sauce through a wire mesh strainer to remove the berry seeds and return the sauce to the pan. Discard the pulp left in the strainer.
10. Reduce the sauce until it is thick and syrupy.
11. Remove the sauce from the heat, and melt the teaspoon of butter into the sauce – Transfer the sauce to a different container and cover to prevent evaporation while waiting for the lamb to be cooked.

12. Remove the lamb racks from the oven and let rest for five minutes to allow meat to retain its juices. Plate by either leaving them whole or by cutting each chop individually.
13. Drizzle the sauce on and around the lamb.

*Makes 2 - 4 servings*

# 16

## Rice is Nice, but Which One to Choose?

Thanks to recent "protein" and "low carb" diets, the awareness of carbohydrate levels is very prevalent in our society. However, starches are slowly making their way back to our dinner tables. Besides pasta and potatoes, rice is always a favorite accompaniment on our plates, and there are many varieties available to us. Are they all so bad?

Ask any dietician and they will most likely tell you that our diets should include a balanced combination of almost all foods... all foods in moderation, that is. Moderation is the key, but when inquiring further, you will realize there is a preference for brown grains verses white. White rice grains are less nutritious because the milling process strips the grain of the bran. Normally when we consume nature made ingredients, they are always more nutritious the closer they are to their original natural state.

**Brown rice** has approximately the same number of calories and carbohydrates as white rice. The difference is brown rice has just the outer husk removed from the rice grain, whereas white rice has the husk and the bran removed. There are a couple of set backs to for the additional health benefits however – it takes twice as long to cook, and it spoils faster in the dry form as it still contains the essential oils of the rice germ.

If eating **white rice** is not a concern for you, then there are a number to choose from: Long grain, short grain, Basmati, Jasmine, etc. Out of all of these options, I normally choose **Basmati** for my busy lifestyle. It cooks the fastest – once the water comes to a boil, cover and simmer for ten to twelve minutes and then serve. It is very fragrant and the delicate grains are a compliment to many rice recipes.

**Short grain** rice is very popular with sushi making. It is mixed with a brine to aid in the binding qualities needed for shaping and to give it distinct sushi rice flavour. For my sushi rice, I dissolve one tablespoon of salt and one-quarter cup of sugar into one third of a cup of rice vinegar, over medium heat. This will make enough to season approximately 3 cups dry short-grain rice, cooked.

**Wild Rice** is a grain that is actually classified as a "grass". When compared to cooked brown and white rice, it offers a lower calories, lower carbohydrates and higher protein. Wild rice is more coarse when served on its own, and therefore is great mixed in combination with other rices.

**Quinoa** (pronounced "keen-wah"), also known as Inca rice, comes from broadleaf plants originally native to the Inca people of South America. It has a somewhat similar appearance to couscous. It offers similar protein and carbohydrate levels as wild rice, a similar calorie count as white or brown rice, but with a higher natural fat content and a nutty flavour. Quinoa can be cooked in the same manner as rice, or cooked without a lid. We sauté the dry grains in olive oil and garlic before adding liquid, and then we stir occasionally, without a lid, until all the liquid is absorbed. If you are tired of serving rice, this makes for a great alternative.

> *Dear Chef Dez:*
>
> *When we are in a hurry, we cook instant rice. How come it can cook so quickly? Is it really rice?*
>
> *Robert P.*
> *South Calgary*

> *Dear Robert:*
>
> *Instant rice is white rice that has been cooked and dehydrated. This allows for faster preparation, but because of the extra processing it offers less nutritional value than raw white rice and is more expensive. For the times when you are in a hurry, I recommend going with Basmati rice, or cook extra rice if you know in advance you are going to be stretched for time.*

# Big Pockets for My Sole

**Full colour photo available at www.chefdez.com**

*"Don't be intimidated by this lengthy recipe. Basically there is 3 parts to making this dish: the sauce, the mushroom & rice filling, and the assembly of the pockets."*

### Hoegaarden Garlic Cream Sauce

2 heads garlic, cloves peeled & left whole (approx. 20-26 cloves)
1 - 330ml bottle Hoegaarden beer (or other light bodied beer)
2 cups whipping cream
1 tsp salt
1 tbsp fresh chopped cilantro

### Wild Rice & Mushroom Filling

½ (one half) cup wild rice, rinsed & drained
1 ½ (one and one half) cups water
½ (one half) tsp salt
2 tbsp canola oil
2 portabella mushrooms, thinly sliced
6 crimini mushrooms, thinly sliced (or regular button mushrooms)
Salt & fresh cracked pepper

### Remaining Ingredients

1 – 397g package frozen puff pastry, thawed (approximately 1 pound)
All purpose flour
1 egg mixed with 1 tbsp water
6 small sole filets
Salt & pepper
2 lemons
Fresh cilantro sprigs
Steamed fiddleheads or asparagus tips

### Sauce Instructions

1. Put garlic cloves and beer in a heavy bottomed medium-sized pot, and bring to a boil over medium heat.
2. Turn the heat down to medium/low and simmer until all the liquid has evaporated, approximately 30 to 40 minutes, stirring occasionally. Be

careful not to burn the garlic. The garlic cloves will become syrupy and coated in the reduced beer.

3. Add the cream and bring to a simmer. At that point, turn down the heat to low and cook for 5 minutes, stirring occasionally.

4. Puree the mixture with a hand-held blender (or in a separate blender or food processor) until the garlic cloves have fully blended into the cream.

5. Add the salt and continue to reduce/thicken over low heat for approximately 5 minutes.

6. Add the chopped cilantro just prior to serving/plating.

## Wild Rice & Mushroom Filling Instructions (make while the sauce is cooking)

1. Stir the rice, water and salt together in a small pot and bring to a boil over high heat.

2. Cover and simmer over low heat for approximately 35 minutes. Strain off excess water through a wire mesh strainer. The wild rice is done when some of the grains have cracked open and it has an "al dente" texture (remember it will also cook in the oven as well). Set aside.

3. Heat a large non-stick pan over medium-high heat. Add the oil and then the mushrooms and season generously with salt and fresh cracked pepper. Sauté until tender, approximately 3 to 5 minutes, stirring occasionally. They will reduce in volume and the liquid from the mushrooms will almost be completely evaporated.

4. Remove from the heat and stir in the cooked wild rice. Taste and re-season with salt & pepper if necessary.

## Assembly & Cooking Instructions

1. Preheat the oven to 400 degrees.

2. Cut pastry into 6 equal portions. On a lightly floured surface, roll out pastry portions into rectangles large enough (approx. 10 x 7 inches) to enclose each piece of fish (filet folded in half). Dusting with extra flour when needed.

3. Lightly season the sole with salt & pepper. Place each piece of fish (folded in half) on a portion of pastry, and top each one with 1/6 (one sixth) of the mushroom/rice mixture.

4. With a pastry brush, moisten all of the edges of the pastry with egg mixture. Enclose each portion by folding up the sides and tucking underneath to completely enclose/seal the sole and filling.

5.   Place sealed pastry pockets on a parchment paper lined baking sheet and lightly brush them with more egg mixture.
6.   Bake for approximately 25 minutes until golden brown.

*Plating Instructions*
On each of the six plates:

1.   Place a mound of seasoned, freshly steamed fiddleheads or asparagus tips on the center of each plate.
2.   Spoon the heated sauce around these mounds.
3.   Gently cut each pocket in half and place on the fiddleheads/asparagus.
4.   Squeeze fresh lemon juice over the entire dish, and top with a lemon slice and some fresh sprigs of cilantro.

*Makes 6 portions*

# Louisiana Red Beans & Rice

**Full colour photo available at www.chefdez.com**
*"One of the staple dishes of New Orleans cooking, and is traditionally eaten on Mondays"*

500g Italian sausage – hot or mild
2 celery stalks, diced small
1 medium onion, diced small
1 medium red bell pepper, diced small
6 garlic cloves, minced
1 tsp dried thyme
1 tsp dried oregano
1 tsp salt
½ (one half) tsp ground black pepper
2 cups long grain white rice
2 – 284ml cans condensed chicken broth
1 ¾ (one and three quarters) cups water
2 bay leaves
1 – 540ml can red kidney beans, rinsed and drained
Fresh thyme, for garnish

1. Squeeze sausages from casings into a large heavy bottomed pot. Discard empty casings.
2. Turn the heat to medium-high and break up sausage meat into small pieces with a wooden spoon while cooking until brown, approximately 10 minutes.
3. Remove sausage with a slotted spoon and set aside, while keeping the sausage fat in the pot.
4. Turn the heat to medium and add the celery, onion, bell pepper, garlic, thyme, oregano, salt and pepper. Cook for approximately 2 to 3 minutes until the vegetables are soft but not brown, stirring occasionally.
5. Add the rice. Stir to coat with the fat and cook approximately 30 seconds until the rice becomes slightly opaque.
6. Add the chicken broth, water and bay leaves. Stir to combine. Turn the heat to high and bring to a boil.
7. Cover with a lid and reduce heat to low and simmer for 20 minutes.
8. Remove the pot from the heat and let stand covered for 5 minutes.
9. Remove and discard the bay leaves. Stir in the beans and the reserved sausage meat.
10. Season with salt and pepper to taste, garnish with fresh thyme sprigs and serve immediately.

*Makes 4 to 6 portions*

# Spanish Paella

12 boneless skinless chicken thighs
Salt & pepper
¼ (one quarter) cup olive oil
340g raw medium prawns, about 30 in total
1 medium white onion, diced small
1 – 398ml can crushed tomatoes
1 tbsp salt
1 tbsp sugar

2 tbsp sweet smoked paprika
6 cups chicken stock
2 bay leaves
2 cups short grain rice
1 cup frozen peas, thawed
1 medium red bell pepper, sliced into ¼ inch strips
3 garlic cloves, minced
2 precooked chorizo sausages (approx.250g), cut into half inch slices/chunks
20 thin asparagus spears, cut into 1 inch pieces

1. Preheat oven to 400 degrees. Season chicken thighs with salt and pepper – bake for 12 minutes and set aside.
2. While chicken is baking, heat a 14-inch paella pan over medium-high heat until hot. Add the oil and once the oil is hot add the prawns. Stirring constantly, cook the prawns until done, approximately 1 minute. Remove from pan with a slotted spoon and set aside.
3. Add the diced onion to the pan and cook until soft and lightly browned, stirring occasionally, approximately 2 to 3 minutes.
4. Stir in the tomatoes, salt, sugar, and paprika.
5. Stir in the chicken stock and bay leaves. Bring to a boil.
6. Add the rice and stir well to distribute evenly. Reduce the heat to medium-low, add the chicken thighs and simmer for 10 minutes.
7. Stir thoroughly to loosen any rice stuck to the bottom of the pan.
8. Stir in the peas, bell pepper, garlic, and sausage. Cook for 20 more minutes, stirring every five minutes to keep the rice from sticking to the bottom of the pan.
9. Taste and re-season if necessary.
10. Add the asparagus and the reserved prawns and cook for 2 more minutes.

*Makes 8 to 10 portions*

# Spicy Coconut Mango Prawns

*"The ingredient "ketjap manis" is basically sweet soy sauce – look for it at your local Asian grocery or down the Asian foods aisle in your major supermarket. If you can't find it you can substitute it with 4 tablespoons of soy sauce mixed with 3 tablespoons of sugar."*

2 tbsp oil
1 medium onion, sliced thin
6 cloves garlic, minced
salt & pepper
4 tbsp ketjap manis
2 tsp sambal oelek
1 cup & 2 tbsp of Pinot Noir or other red wine
1 tbsp & 1 tsp cornstarch
2 mangos, pitted, peeled, & diced
1 large yellow bell pepper, julienne cut
1.5 lbs fresh or 1-680g bag frozen raw large prawns, thawed & drained
cooked rice
½ (one half) cup sweet grated coconut
3 – 5 green onions, sliced diagonally

1. Heat a large heavy bottomed pan or wok over medium high heat.
2. Add the oil, onion, and garlic. Season with salt & pepper and sauté for 1 minute.
3. Add 2 tbsp of the ketjap manis and the sambal oelek, and sauté for 1 more minute until the onions are soft.
4. Add the 1 cup of wine, and bring to a boil over high heat. Meanwhile, mix the 2 tbsp of wine with the cornstarch.
5. Once boiling, stir the cornstarch mixture, and add the mango, bell pepper, and prawns. Cook for approximately 1 to 2 minutes until the prawns are just cooked through and the sauce has thickened. Do not over cook!
6. Stir in the remaining 2 tbsp of ketjap manis, and serve over warm, seasoned cooked rice.
7. Garnish with grated coconut and green onion slices.

*Serves 4 to 6 people.*

# Swedish Cabbage Rolls

*"Special thanks to Wendy for the base of this recipe"*

8 large green cabbage leaves
227g (1/2 pound) lean ground beef
227g (1/2 pound) lean ground pork
¾ (three quarters) cup cooked rice
2/3 (two thirds) cup milk
¼ (one quarter) cup finely chopped onion
1 egg
1 clove garlic, finely chopped
1 ½ (one and one half) tsp salt
1 tsp Worcestershire sauce
¼ (one quarter) tsp sambal oelek
Pinch of pepper

<u>Sauce Ingredients</u>
1 – 398ml can of diced tomatoes, drained well
1 – 284ml can of condensed tomato soup
2 tbsp minced onion
1 tbsp dark brown sugar
1 tbsp Worcestershire sauce
1 tbsp cornstarch

More salt & pepper
1 tbsp cold butter, broken into small bits
Sour cream, for serving

1.  Carefully remove the eight leaves from the cabbage without breaking them by first coring out the bottom of the cabbage as much as possible. Cut out the thickest center part of the rib of each leaf – approximately 1 to 2 inches worth. Steam the leaves over boiling water for approximately 4 minutes until soft. Set the leaves aside to drain in a colander.
2.  Preheat the oven to 350 degrees.

3. In a bowl, thoroughly combine the beef, pork, rice, milk, onion, egg, garlic, salt, Worcestershire, sambal oelek and pepper together. Score the top of the mixture to mark 8 equal portions of this mixture.

4. Put one portion in each of the cabbage leaves. Roll up the sides of the leaf around the meat mixture and roll up towards the bottom part of the leaf where the rib was cut out. Repeat with the other 7 leaves and place them tightly together in a 9 x 9 size casserole dish.

5. Mix the sauce ingredients together and pour evenly over the cabbage rolls. Sprinkle with salt, pepper and the small bits of butter. Bake for 1 hour, and then let sit for 15-20 minutes before serving with dollops of sour cream.

*Makes 8 large cabbage rolls*

CHEF DEZ

# 17

## *Umami: The Fifth Taste*

We have all seen the commercials on TV of a leading soy sauce company utilizing the term "Umami", but not surrendering any substantial information as to what exactly umami is.

Eating is a celebration of the senses. All five of them in fact: taste, smell, sight, touch, and sound. Keeping this in mind, there could be an argument in deciding as to which is the most important sense when it comes to eating. They all play significant roles in the symphony of eating, but "taste" is the one that the majority of people associate with the most when it comes to the enjoyment of their favorite dish or cuisine.

Upon further examination of the "taste" sense, we are able to break it down into four recognizable basic distinctions: sweet, sour, salty and bitter. This dissection however does not capture the taste of such things as steak, potatoes, prawns, asparagus, tuna, and mushrooms for example. In each of these mentioned instances we can recognize that there is a distinct taste to all of these ingredients, but none of them fall into the four previously stated categories of taste. How would you describe the taste of a steak besides using an uncreative term such as "meaty"? This is where umami comes in.

The commercial on TV mentions that umami is Japanese for delicious, but the definition has much more depth than that. Umami is the recognition of a pleasant savoury taste that has been impacted by naturally occurring amino acids in food usually signaling the presence of protein. No combination of sweet, sour, salty or bitter can replicate or mimic the taste of umami, and thus it is a basic taste description all in its own. I like to translate that it represents the heartiness in the taste of something.

The science of taste suggests that we have these five basic taste senses for a reason. Sweet indicates to our body a source of energy and carbohydrates, salty a source of minerals, sour as evidence that something is not ripe, bitter as a signal that a toxin may be present, and umami signifying protein, an important part of human health.

The culinary world can be so enjoyable and is an integral part of our day to day lives, however every day many people eat unconsciously without thinking about the senses that we experience while eating. In fact there are many books and theories about this as the assumption as to why there are increasing numbers in obesity in today's society.

What ever the case may be, the next time you lift your fork to your mouth, stop, close your eyes and relish everything each bite offers your awaiting palate. You may just find umami everywhere your appetite takes you.

# Baked Chicken Fingers

*"An easy kid friendly recipe. Healthier than deep frying and a great lesson on breading."*

16 chicken breast filets
¼ (one quarter) cup flour
Salt & pepper
2 eggs
2 tablespoons cold water
1 cup breadcrumbs

1. Preheat oven to 425 degrees.
2. Spray a baking sheet with baking spray.
3. Mix the flour with some salt and pepper on a large plate.
4. In a bowl, whisk the eggs and water together.
5. Pour the breadcrumbs onto another large plate.
6. Take each filet and roll it in the seasoned flour. Dunk it in the egg mixture and roll it in the breadcrumbs. Place it on the prepared baking sheet. Repeat this for all of the chicken filets.
7. Bake for 13 – 15 minutes and serve with any or all the "no-cook sauces".

# Honey Mustard Sauce

½ (one half) cup Mayonnaise
1 tablespoon yellow mustard
1 tablespoon liquid honey

1. Mix together and keep refrigerated.

# Cajun Grilled Flank Steak with Grits

**Full colour photo available at www.chefdez.com**

*"Grits are traditionally made with ground Hominy, but since this is not readily available I have substituted it with fine cornmeal."*

### Steak Ingredients
¼ (one quarter) cup paprika
2 tsp ground black pepper
2 tsp ground dried oregano
2 tsp salt
½ - 1 tsp cayenne pepper
1 – 600g-700g beef flank steak

### Garlic Butter (mix together)
4 tbsp melted butter
1 garlic clove, crushed
1 tsp finely chopped parsley

### Grits Ingredients
2 cups water
2 tsp salt
2 cups milk
7 tbsp butter, cubed small
1 cup fine cornmeal

100g Montery Jack cheese, grated
2 – 3 garlic cloves, crushed

1. In a small bowl, combine the paprika, pepper, oregano, salt, and cayenne. Liberally coat the steak with this mixture and let sit in the refrigerator for at least 1 hour.
2. Preheat BBQ grill. Cook the flank steak for approximately 5 – 7 minutes per side, with the lid open, over medium-high heat for medium-rare to medium doneness – depending on the thickness of the steak.
3. Let rest for 2 – 3 minutes before slicing to help retain the juiciness of the meat.
4. Once the steak has rested, slice the steak across the grain into thin strips.
5. Serve each plate with a dollop of grits topped with strips of flank steak and drizzled with 1 tablespoon of garlic butter.

_Prepare the grits while the steak is grilling:_

1. In a heavy bottomed pot, bring the water and salt to a boil over high heat.
2. Add the milk and butter and stir until the butter has melted into the liquid.
3. Turn the heat to low and add the cornmeal gradually while whisking.
4. Simmer, while whisking constantly, for approximately 3 – 5 minutes until mixture has thickened.
5. Stir in the cheese gradually and stir in the garlic.
6. Remove from heat, cover, and set aside until the steak is ready to serve.

_Makes 4 servings_

# Rumbledethumps

**Full colour photo available at www.chefdez.com**

_"A classic Scottish side dish. Very economical."_

4 extra-large russet potatoes, peeled and diced one-half inch
5 cups shredded (or thinly sliced) green cabbage
1 small onion, diced small
6 large cloves of garlic, minced

¾ (three quarters) cup butter
4 tsp salt
1 tsp pepper
¾ (three quarters) cup whipping cream
1 cup grated old cheddar
Fresh chopped parsley, for garnish

1. Steam the diced potatoes over boiling water until tender, approximately 20 minutes.
2. Preheat the oven to 350 degrees.
3. While the potatoes are steaming, melt ¼ (one quarter) cup of the butter in a large pan over medium heat until it just starts foaming. Add the cabbage, onion, garlic and 1 tsp of the salt to the pan and cook until mostly soft, while stirring occasionally. Approximately 15 minutes.
4. Cube the remaining ½ (one half) cup butter and add it to the steamed potatoes along with the other 3 tsp salt and the 1 tsp pepper. Mash until thoroughly combined.
5. Stir the cabbage mixture, whipping cream, and ½ (one half) cup of the grated cheddar into the potatoes until thoroughly combined. Taste and re-season if necessary.
6. Transfer to a baking dish, top with the remaining cheddar and parsley, and bake for 20 minutes.

*Make approximately 6 to 10 side portions*

# Scotch Eggs

**Full colour photo available at www.chefdez.com**

*"A classic and popular Scottish appetizer... or great as a snack or breakfast too!"*

1 cup soda cracker crumbs
½ (one half) cup minced fresh parsley
6 hard boiled eggs
454g (1 pound) pork breakfast sausages

1. Preheat oven to 375 degrees
2. Mix the cracker crumbs and the parsley together in a shallow dish.
3. Peel the eggs. Squeeze the sausage meat from the casings and discard the casings. Encase each of the peeled eggs in an equal amount of the sausage meat.
4. Roll each of the sausage coated eggs in the crumb/parsley mixture. Place on a baking sheet and bake for 30-35 minutes until the sausage meat is cooked through, turning occasionally.
5. Store in refrigerator until ready to serve. Cut each egg into 4 wedges for serving.

*Makes 24 wedges*


# Taco Fried Steak with Fresh Guacamole

*"A twist on chicken fried steak. This was a "cowboy" recipe I did for the Cloverdale Rodeo"*

<u>Guacamole Ingredients</u>
2 soft avocados
Juice from 1 large lime
¼ (one quarter) yellow bell pepper, finely diced
¼ (one quarter) red bell pepper, finely diced
¼ (one quarter) red onion, finely diced
½ (one half) jalapeno pepper, minced
1 garlic clove, crushed

½ (one half) tsp ground cumin
½ (one half) tsp sambal oelek
½ (one half) tsp sugar
Salt & pepper, to taste

*Other Ingredients*
4 eye of round steaks, pounded thin
1 pkg. taco seasoning
5 tbsp flour
3 eggs
¼ (one quarter) cup milk
1 ½ (one and one half) cups cornflake crumbs
3 tbsp canola oil
3 tbsp butter
Sour Cream & chopped parsley, for garnish

1.  Cut, pit, and peel the avocados. Mash them in a medium bowl with the lime juice. Add all of the other guacamole ingredients to the bowl and mix together. Refrigerate until needed.
2.  Mix the taco seasoning and the flour on a large plate.
3.  Whisk the eggs and the milk together in a bowl large enough to hold a steak.
4.  Pour the cornflake crumbs onto a large plate.
5.  Coat the steaks individually by tossing them in the seasoned flour, then in the egg wash, and then rolling them in the cornflake crumbs.
6.  Heat a heavy bottomed nonstick pan over medium to medium-high heat and melt the butter into the oil. When hot, add the breaded steaks to the pan. Fry the steaks on each side until golden brown, approximately 3 to 5 minutes per side.
7.  Carefully remove the steaks from the pan, and plate them individually with a large dollop of guacamole in the center, a smaller dollop of sour cream on the guacamole, and then a sprinkle of parsley.

*Makes 4 portions*

# *Glossary of Terms*

**Al denté** – Italian for *"to the tooth"*. The term most commonly used to describe the cooking of pasta, meaning it should not be overcooked and have a bit of resistance when bitten into.

**Baguette** – a long thin French loaf of bread.

**Beef Stock Paste** – beef stock/broth that has been concentrated down to a paste consistency. Allows one to add intense flavour without adding liquid to a recipe.

**Bruscetta** – toasted slices of baguette topped with a variety of ingredients and served as an appetizer.

**Cheesecloth** – originally used to separate curds from the whey in cheese making, this food-safe perforated cloth has numerous filtering uses in the kitchen.

**Chicken Stock Paste** – chicken stock/broth that has been concentrated down to a paste consistency. Allows one to add intense flavour without adding liquid to a recipe.

**Chipotle Peppers** – are smoked jalapeno peppers and are usually packaged in cans.

**Deglaze** – to remove the browned bits (fond) in a hot pan by adding a liquid. This lifts the fond off of the pan and it becomes part of the sauce/finished dish.

**Demiglaze** – technically speaking this should be a combination of half brown sauce with half brown stock and then reduced in volume by half. Now-a-days this term is loosely used in a number of different recipes meaning a reduced sauce.

**Double Boiler** – a pot or saucepan that has an insert that sits above the water level. This allows to cook with steam as a heat source.

**Dredge** – to drag through dry ingredients to coat.

**Emulsifier** – an ingredient, such as egg yolks, that helps bind oil and liquids together.

**Frenched Rack of Lamb** – bones on the rack have been cleaned of tissue/fat for better presentation.

**Ketjap Manis** – is basically sweet soy sauce. Look for it at your local Asian grocery or down the Asian foods aisle in your major supermarket. If you can't find it you can substitute it with 4 tablespoons of soy sauce mixed with 3 tablespoons of sugar.

**Melon Baller** – a kitchen utensil that has a half sphere stainless steel end that is commonly used to create round balls of solid fruits like melons.

**Reduce/Reduction** – to decrease in volume by the process of evaporation. As steam rises from a pan/pot, water is being released and the residual product has intensified flavour and is smaller in quantity.

**Sambal Oelek** – a crushed chili product that comes in a liquid/paste form. It can usually be found in any major grocery store down the Asian food isle or Imported foods isle.

**Shallot** – a variety of onion that is smaller and milder than regular onions.

**tbsp** – abbreviation for tablespoon.

**tsp** - abbreviation for teaspoon.

**Tzatziki** – a Greek dipping sauce made from yogurt, cucumber, fresh dill and garlic. Traditionally served on Greek souvlaki.

**Vegetable Stock Paste** – vegetable stock/broth that has been concentrated down to a paste consistency. Allows one to add intense flavour without adding liquid to a recipe.

**White Pepper** – is ground peppercorns that have been allowed to mature before harvesting. They are then either soaked or washed in water to remove the outer shell, which produces a white peppercorn with a milder taste. They are frequently utilized to season white sauces to ensure that the appearance of the sauce is not marred with black specs.

**Zest** – the coloured outer peel of citrus fruit, not the white bitter pith on the underside of the peel. A tool called a zester or a fine-toothed food grater will help remove this efficiently.

## Appetizers

## Beef

# L

# M

# P

## R

## Rice

## S

## Salads

CHEF DEZ

## Soups/Stews

## Spreads/Dips

## Volume measurements

| | | |
|---|---|---|
| 3 teaspoons | = | 1 tablespoon |
| 2 tablespoons | = | 1 fluid ounce |
| 2 fluid ounces | = | ¼ (one quarter) cup |
| ¼ (one quarter) cup | = | 4 tablespoons |
| 8 fluid ounces | = | 1 cup or 16 tablespoons |
| 1 litre | = | 4 cups or 32 fluid ounces |

## Weight Measurements

| | | |
|---|---|---|
| 227 grams | = | ½ (one half) pound |
| 454 grams | = | 1 pound |
| 1 pound | = | 16 ounces (not fluid ounces) |
| 1 kilogram | = | 2.2 pounds |

## Oven Temperature Measurements (Fahrenheit to Celsius)

| | | |
|---|---|---|
| 225 degrees F | = | 105 degrees C |
| 250 degrees F | = | 120 degrees C |
| 275 degrees F | = | 135 degrees C |
| 300 degrees F | = | 150 degrees C |
| 325 degrees F | = | 165 degrees C |
| 350 degrees F | = | 175 degrees C |
| 375 degrees F | = | 190 degrees C |
| 400 degrees F | = | 205 degrees C |
| 425 degrees F | = | 220 degrees C |
| 450 degrees F | = | 230 degrees C |
| 475 degrees F | = | 245 degrees C |